LIFTOFF!

The Tank, the Storm, and the Astros'
Improbable Ascent to Baseball Immortality

Brian T. Smith

TRIUMPH
BOOKS

This book is available in quantity at special discounts for your group or organization. For further information, contact:

Triumph Books LLC
814 North Franklin Street
Chicago, IL 60610
(312) 337-0747
www.triumphbooks.com

Printed in the United States of America

ISBN: 978-1-62937-623-3
Design and editorial production by Alex Lubertozzi
All photos courtesy of AP Images

This book is dedicated to my wife and parents

CONTENTS

AUTHOR'S NOTE

We never lost perspective of what was important. I saw these guys at the community center....I saw these guys do good deeds for people as they start to rebuild the city. And I think that's why the city fell in love with this team all over again, and why we had that Houston Strong strength that carried us a long way.
—Astros manager A.J. Hinch

THEY WERE THE worst team in baseball. Not even worth watching. As bad as anything the city had ever seen and one of the biggest embarrassments in the history of major league baseball.

They became the best team in baseball. Instantly and constantly addicting. Loaded with names, faces, and stories people loved. True winners in a city that needed new hope. World champions during a year when it felt like everything was suddenly falling apart.

José Altuve.

George Springer.

Carlos Correa.

Justin Verlander, Dallas Keuchel, Alex Bregman, and A.J. Hinch.

Jeff Luhnow, the architect of it all. Jim Crane, who went from the most-loathed owner in Houston's thriving pro sports scene to the man venerated for the construction of a World Series winner in just six years. For a while, those years felt like decades. For Houston, the wait from 1962 to 2017 almost felt like forever.

Then you throw in the chaos and destruction of Hurricane Harvey; the depressing, lonely, 100-loss seasons when the "Lastros" were the annual laughingstock of MLB; all the names and faces that just kept changing and changing and changing...all in the name of a rebuild that took years just to reach rock bottom. The painful collapse in Game 4 of the 2015 American League Division Series against the eventual world-champion Kansas City Royals. The fact that, when the reconstructed Astros finally did make their first real moves at the trade deadline, they really did not get any better. And then when everyone knew they were maybe just a few names away two years later, the team waited until absolutely the last minute to finally wrap Verlander in orange and blue.

So when it all came together after waiting 56 years? Of course, it felt and looked like brilliant, perfect magic.

I am typing this three months later and I still find myself struggling to believe it.

All the T-shirts that you still see everywhere say, "World Champions." The hats, stickers, photos, and newspaper reprints—and everything else that displays lasting, indisputable proof of the winners of the 2017 World Series—now woven into this winning city.

But then I randomly think back to some forgotten name or horrendous game from the 111-loss 2013 team, and I have another one of those moments. The rebuild was real—massive and unforgiving. The tear-down. The reconstruction. Blowing it all up, digging down so deep, betting everything on proving almost everyone wrong...and then taking Mark Appel over Kris Bryant during the same year they lost 111 games.

Those Astros really won the World Series?

They sure as heck did.

Because of Altuve, Springer, Correa, Verlander, Keuchel, and Bregman. Because Hinch was the perfect fit and voice from day one. Because the plan kept evolving, Luhnow kept adapting, Crane stepped up when he had to, and the Astros really were as smart and forward-thinking as they acted.

But, really, it all came down to heart, personal drive, and natural talent that just kept being refined. And for all the numbers, statistics, projections, advanced analytics, defensive shifts, and everything else that has absolutely altered the grand old game, the 2017 Astros were also the best team in baseball—with an emphasis on "team."

They loved to play baseball. So much that they refused to stop. From early February in sunny West Palm Beach, Florida, to November 1 in the glowing, electric Los Angeles night at Dodger Stadium, when a relentless team that was still ahead of schedule ended the season of the highest-priced club in the game.

The rebuilt Astros were simply better—and more fun.

Altuve playing his heart out, proudly covered in dirt. Springer refusing to fail, then not believing what he was seeing. Bregman acting like a 23-year-old but playing like he was 30. Verlander and Keuchel challenging everyone around them to keep fighting, after both had already placed the team on their backs. Hinch always so calm and cool, but also fueled by a fire that guided his Astros to a final stage reserved only for champions.

They took a wrecking ball to it all and said that maybe one day there would be a trophy. No promises, because that is just how baseball goes. Then they built a team that won your hearts, honored a recovering city, and will last as long as baseball does.

From 111 losses to 101 wins. Through the Boston Red Sox, New York Yankees, and Los Angeles Dodgers. Into your lives forever.

The once horrible, then amazing, Houston Astros.

Liftoff.

Timeline—Countdown to Liftoff

July 20, 2011: José Altuve makes his major league debut at Minute Maid Park, going 1-for-5 as the Astros fall to 33–65.

September 28, 2011: Six years after Houston appears in its first World Series—a 4-0 defeat to the Chicago White Sox—the Astros finish 56–106, worst in major league baseball.

November 17, 2011: MLB approves Jim Crane's purchase of the Astros. With the sale, Houston is set to move to the American League.

December 7, 2011: The Astros hire Jeff Luhnow as general manager. He begins an unprecedented organizational rebuild.

June 4, 2012: The Astros select shortstop Carlos Correa with the No. 1 overall pick in MLB's amateur draft. Pitcher Lance McCullers Jr. is later taken at No. 41.

August 18, 2012: Houston fires manager Brad Mills. The Astros finish 55–107 and are again the worst team in baseball.

September 27, 2012: Bo Porter, then third-base coach for the Washington Nationals, is hired as Houston's new manager.

March 31, 2013: The Astros beat the Texas Rangers 8–2 at Minute Maid Park in their AL debut. The Opening Day victory is the only time all season the Astros are above .500.

June 6, 2013: The Astros select pitcher Mark Appel with the No. 1 pick in the draft. The Chicago Cubs take third baseman Kris Bryant at No. 2.

July 14, 2013: Houston enters the All-Star break at 33–61. The team's active payroll soon drops below $15 million.

September 29, 2013: The Astros lose 15 straight games to end the season, amassing a franchise-record 111 losses with only 51 wins. Houston has the worst record in MLB for the third year in a row.

April 16, 2014: Outfielder George Springer, the No. 11 pick of the 2011 draft, makes his major league debut for the Astros.

September 1, 2014: On the way to a 70–92 record, a fourth-place finish in the AL West, and sixth straight losing season, the Astros fire Porter. He finishes with a 110–190 mark in Houston.

September 28, 2014: Altuve wins his first MLB batting crown, hitting .341 for the season.

September 29, 2014: A.J. Hinch is named the Astros' new manager.

April 30, 2015: Houston goes 15–7 during its first month under Hinch. The Astros reach 34–20 in early June before a seven-game losing streak.

June 8, 2015: Correa makes his major league debut for the Astros. On the same day, Houston selects infielder Alex Bregman with the No. 2 pick in the draft. (McCullers debuted on May 18.)

October 4, 2015: Despite going 11–16 in September and losing their final game of the regular season, the Astros clinch their first postseason appearance in a decade during Game 162. Houston finishes 86–76 in its first season under Hinch, two games behind the Rangers for first place in the AL West.

October 12, 2015: After beating New York 3–0 in a wild-card game at Yankee Stadium, the Astros hold a 2–1 AL Division Series lead against Kansas City and are up 6–2 as the eighth inning begins during Game 4 at Minute Maid Park. The Royals score five runs in the eighth and win 9–6. The eventual World Series champion Royals close out the ALDS with a 7–2 win in Kansas City two days later, ending the Astros' season.

November 16, 2015: Correa wins the AL Rookie of the Year award. Dallas Keuchel is honored with the AL Cy Young Award two days later.

May 22, 2016: A backward 7–17 start turns into a 17–28 beginning, following a three-game sweep by the Rangers. Despite going 35–20 combined during May and June, the Astros never fully recover from their early-season hole

October 2, 2016: The Rangers win the AL West for the second consecutive season, buoyed by key midseason trades. The Astros finish 84–78 during their second year under Hinch, just two games off their 2015 mark, but third place in the division and out of the playoffs.

December 5, 2016: Carlos Beltran, a postseason hero for the 2004 Astros and trade-deadline acquisition for the 2016 Rangers, agrees to a one-year deal with Houston. The Beltran signing follows a trade for Brian McCann and long-term deal for Josh Reddick, as the Astros add respected veterans to a deepened lineup.

June 1, 2017: A 16–9 April is followed by a 22–7 May. The Astros begin 2017 as the best team in baseball and hold an 11½-game lead in the AL West.

July 11, 2017: Houston sends a team-record six players to the All-Star Game: Altuve, Chris Devenski, Keuchel, McCullers, Correa, and Springer. Five were drafted or initially signed by the Astros.

August 31, 2017: Houston acquires veteran right-hander Justin Verlander from the Detroit Tigers minutes before MLB's final trade deadline expires.

September 2, 2017: The Astros play a home game in Houston for the first time since Hurricane Harvey, sweeping the New York Mets in a doubleheader at Minute Maid Park.

September 17, 2017: Verlander strikes out 10 and only allows one run during seven innings against Seattle. The Astros win the American League West before their home crowd, four seasons after switching leagues and moving to the AL.

October 21, 2017: After beating the Boston Red Sox 3–1 in the AL Division Series, the Astros fight off two elimination games to down the Yankees 4–3 in Game 7 of the AL Championship Series and win the pennant.

November 1, 2017: The Astros defeat the Los Angeles Dodgers 5–1 in Game 7 of the World Series at Dodger Stadium to take the series 4–3. Springer is named World Series MVP.

March 19, 2018: Altuve, the 2017 AL MVP, signs a five-year, $151 million contract extension with the Astros. It is the largest contract in team history.

1

HERE WE GO

It's a crazy journey, man. But I think I was the only one in 2011, '12, and '13, those hundred losses, three years in a row. It's not easy. But I kind of believed in the process. I believed in what Jeff Luhnow and Jim Crane used to talk to me, "Hey, we're going to be good. We're going to be good." Then, okay, let me keep working hard. Let me get better every year and try to be part of the winning team.

—Astros second baseman José Altuve

IT IS 2015, and they are tired of losing.

Two managers have been fired. A team president has departed. Names are going to keep revolving, but a few players are actually going to stick around in Houston, and one of them wants more than this.

Losing. Losing. Losing.

Enough.

José Altuve enters the office of the Astros' new manager. Altuve was never supposed to make it in major league baseball. Now he's one of the best hitters in the game. In three seasons, he will hit three home runs in a single playoff game, win the American League MVP award, and cement himself as the franchise face of a World Series winner. But in 2015? Altuve only wants to do the one thing he has never done in the majors: win.

The manager who will soon become so close with and trusted by his players—who will guide the Astros to 101 victories and through two playoff Game 7s; loudest vote in the clubhouse, calmest heart-beat in the dugout—listens and immediately gets it.

A.J. Hinch came to Houston to win. He became the Astros' next manager because the team had to stop losing. What Altuve has been feeling, Hinch already is, too. And soon the new manager will show the whole team the Astros' new world order. "When I got here no one talked about winning," Hinch said. "And that was one of the first things that Altuve told me in my office, that he wanted to win. And that represented what the next step was for this organization."

It is 2017, just four years after the worst team in franchise history went 51–111. An unprecedented rebuild peaks in Game 7 of the World Series, during a Fall Classic that instantly becomes one of the best in the sport's history.

Justin Verlander wanted to join the Astros. The Boston Red Sox have fallen, the New York Yankees went down, and the Los Angeles Dodgers could not match the Astros' heart.

Houston's baseball team is saturated with young stars who will still be around the next season—the free-agency blues have not set in yet. The Astros now spend enough money to play the big game, but are also set up for years, and prime talent is still flowing through the pipeline. Many MLB clubs would do anything just to have Altuve in uniform. The Astros have Carlos Correa, George Springer, Alex Bregman, Altuve, and more.

Houston is a baseball town again. Minute Maid Park has roared. And two winners share the same stage inside Dodger Stadium, answering constant questions about what it all feels like.

"I always believed that we're going to become good," Altuve said. "Then I saw Springer get drafted, Correa and Bregman, and I was like, 'Okay, here we go.'"

They were going to win more than they ever had before.

But first the Astros had to lose. A lot.

2

THIS CITY DESERVES OUR BEST

We laid the foundation. And it takes years to lay the right foundation. It's like building a house. You want to make sure... that your foundation isn't cracked. That you've got the right foundation, so that as you build on top of it, you can sustain a lot of growth on top of it. And that's really what we're doing at all the levels.

—Astros general manager Jeff Luhnow

THERE WOULD BE much brighter days. There would also be dates that would come to define the rebuilt Astros—months, numbers, and years that proudly became part of franchise history.

April 16, 2014: George Springer makes his major league baseball debut.

October 4, 2015: Led by manager A.J. Hinch, the Astros make the playoffs for the first time in a decade.

July 25, 2016: Alex Bregman debuts.

August 31, 2017: Justin Verlander is traded to the Astros.

November 1, 2017: The Houston Astros win their first World Series, beating Los Angeles in Game 7 at Dodger Stadium.

But December 7, 2011, was the start of it all. It was when the full reconstruction began. New owner Jim Crane placed the Astros in Jeff Luhnow's hands, hiring the former vice president of scouting and player development for the St. Louis Cardinals and naming

Luhnow as Houston's new general manager. Since 2003 Luhnow had risen through the Cardinals organization. In 2011 one of baseball's most storied franchises had won the World Series again, downing the Texas Rangers in a seven-game series. An Astros teardown that began under former GM Ed Wade—who was fired, along with team president Tal Smith, on November 27, 2011— would now begin in full under Luhnow.

As the Astros slid through the post–Craig Biggio and Jeff Bagwell era, below .500 seasons piled up and the farm system dried up. The franchise had not made the playoffs since its first-ever World Series run in 2005, and it required the team trading away its remaining stars (Roy Oswalt, Lance Berkman, Hunter Pence, Michael Bourn) for Astros fans to even begin to see a murky future. Still, the minor leagues were not barren: Springer, the 2017 World Series MVP, was taken No. 11 overall in the 2011 MLB amateur draft. José Altuve, the 2017 American League MVP, had made his major league debut on July 20, 2011, and 2015 AL Cy Young winner Dallas Keuchel had been taken in the seventh round of the 2009 draft.

The Astros went 56–106 in 2011 under manager Brad Mills. Their final game was an 8–0 home loss to the Cardinals before 24,358 fans at Minute Maid Park. The 1–9 names: J.B. Shuck, Altuve, J.D. Martinez (who would hit 45 home runs in 2017 and receive a $110 million contract from the Boston Red Sox in 2018), Carlos Lee, Brian Bogusevic, Jimmy Paredes, Clint Barmes, Humberto Quintero, and Brett Myers. Not exactly world beaters.

The team went 55–107 during Luhnow's first year, as Mills was fired, Lee was traded, and the names kept coming and going. But by October 2012, the GM believed he was watching a plan slowly come together, while outside critics thought they were only witnessing destruction.

How would Luhnow fix Houston's broken baseball team? Was it truly possible to revive and rebuild the Astros? How do you turn 213 losses in two seasons into a clubhouse loaded with consistent winners and a youth movement that long-frustrated fans wanted to buy into?

Of course, Luhnow had a vision. A team that was part *Moneyball* Oakland Athletics and Tampa Bay Rays, part big-city Los Angeles Dodgers and Rangers. A club that grew internally and developed its own talent, but could also spend big money when it needed to.

During the early years, the Astros' propensity for losing games was only rivaled by the franchise's intent on cleaning house. Familiar names were gone. New uniforms containing throwback colors and images were unveiled. Minute Maid Park was upgraded. Most importantly, as the Astros' major league roster hit financial and statistical rock bottom, a once-depleted farm system was being restocked.

An unprecedented rebuild was fully underway.

"We'd like to [watch] it go as fast as it can without making promises on any time frame," Luhnow said in October 2012. "This city deserves a baseball team that they're not only proud of, they're excited to come to the ballpark and watch. And I don't think we're that far away from being able to deliver."

Gradually torn down and remade, the Astros began emphasizing improved player promotion guidelines—only promoting a prospect when his play and development merited reward—while deepening the international talent pipeline and reconfiguring roles and departments. Minor league affiliates were streamlined, and winning was emphasized there first. By the time a young athlete arrived in the majors, they would be used to daily victories and winning the right way.

"One of the things that we're doing here—and I think we're going to do exceptionally well—is linking everything together so there are no [breaks]. The guy who runs international feels like he's connected to the front office," Luhnow said. "Everybody has their area of expertise. But the more we can be sharing experiences and collaborating on things, I think the more we can be better as a team."

But how long would the rebuild take? Two years? Five? What if the blueprint failed, and the Astros—the worst team in baseball for two consecutive seasons—became the next Pittsburgh Pirates, reaching a hard ceiling, then tearing it down and rebuilding all over again?

"You compare our roster to the Rangers', we're not there yet. But will we be in five years? I hope so. Will our payroll be up in the range where it can compete with the Rangers? I hope so," Luhnow said. "But for now, we're not even close. So we know we have our work cut out for us. I think what'll be fun for our fans is to experience the cycle on the way up. Our fans have gone through the painful experience of the cycle on the way down, from the World Series in 2005 to basically two 100-loss seasons in a row. This is as far down as it goes. From here, going forward, it goes up."

To slowly build upward, the Astros drastically changed almost everything. Players, staffs, scouts, TV faces, and radio voices, long-time employees...the team colors, logos, and even the mascot. By 2015 Minute Maid Park would feel like a completely new place, and the on-field product would be worlds beyond the 2012 team. But Luhnow also relied on several key, lasting names—Mike Elias, Kevin Goldstein, Sig Mejdal, Oz Ocampo, Mike Fast—within the franchise's remade baseball operations side. Hires initially questioned by some became critical components to the rebuild. In 2015 a Milwaukee franchise trying to return to .500 ball and then the playoffs hired 30-year-old David Stearns—who had worked closely with Luhnow from 2012 to 2015 as the Astros' assistant general manager—as the Brewers' next GM.

Still, the early years were an awkward balance for the Astros—and that is putting it nicely. There were social-media blunders, stadium embarrassments, and an insulting on-field product that only got worse. By September 2014, a much-hyped manager would be coldly replaced, while the team president/CEO would have already resigned and also be replaced. The franchise dug down so deep that the only way to make the reconstruction worth all the pain was a World Series trophy. There was also a coldness to the initial stages of the rebuild—arrogant and dismissive, calculating and even ruthless—that only fed into a belief that the Astros were running a baseball team like a modern business experiment and building a big-league club the wrong way.

Most pro organizations put on a warm public face, then are calculating and all business behind closed doors. The Astros regularly asked for patience as their plan unfolded and explained the lengths they were going to, to fully turn the franchise around. But by tearing everything down to ground level, they also put their business on the table.

The recurring word from 2011 to 2014: assets.

"Major league value, that's the objective, that's what we're trying to produce," Luhnow said. "And the way you produce that is you acquire these assets—whether it's through the draft or through trades—that have the possibility of becoming that. And then you need to set up a system so you can constantly acquire these things as well or better than your competition. So what does that mean? It means having good scouts and good processes for identifying the universe of talent that's out there that you might bring in. Being good at negotiating and doing the right deals to get it in. And then having the right pieces to help build it."

Luhnow used a manufacturing analogy about "raw material" and referred to the Astros being in a "zero-sum game."

It was not all about green grass, an open field, and the classic crack of a bat. It also was not just about outsmarting the game.

"A win for us is a loss for someone else," said Luhnow, whose unique background included general manager and vice president of marketing at Petstore.com and work with a global management consulting firm, graduating from the University of Pennsylvania with degrees in economics and engineering, and earning an MBA from the Kellogg School of Management at Northwestern University.

"There's certain things where the industry gets smarter and better as a whole. But we're still competing with one another on a daily basis, so our advantage needs to come at someone else's disadvantage," Luhnow said. "So we're always looking to gain an edge. And it's not just in one area. You can gain an edge in 50 different areas that add up to a meaningful edge. And in some you're going to have a deficiency because of your market or your current situation."

The heart would eventually be everywhere on the field: a fun, lovable, addicting team led by Carlos Correa, Altuve, and Springer.

The Astros' first critical step forward began in the 2012 draft. Corey Seager went to Los Angeles at No. 18 overall. Addison Russell was drafted by Oakland at No. 11, then eventually traded to the rebuilding Chicago Cubs. Marcus Stroman went to Toronto at 22. But in a draft that would not stand out as an all-timer years later, the rapidly changing Astros made two crucial selections that would come to define their new era.

Correa was taken No. 1 overall on June 4 as a 17-year-old shortstop out of the Puerto Rico Baseball Academy. Opting for Correa instead of outfielder Byron Buxton (Minnesota, No. 2) or a collection of college pitchers, the Astros made a selection that would come to capture the all-in nature of their rebuild. They could be criticized and picked apart from the outside. But within their franchise, they had a vision and they were sticking to it.

When high school pitcher Lance McCullers Jr. was taken at No. 41 overall in the supplemental round, the Astros collected two key names who would be hoisting a World Series trophy just five years later.

On the major league field, though, the Astros were a disaster and only getting worse. The "Lastros" were laughable.

Houston's baseball team drew 3,087,872 fans in 2004, ranking seventh in MLB in home attendance. By 2012, the total number had almost been cut in half (1,607,733), and the Astros ranked 28th out of 30 teams. Tickets were a struggle to give away. Fans knew the season was over before it began, and a new TV regional sports network became an albatross, limiting viewership and further alienating already turned-off supporters. The rebuilding Astros were not worth watching—and it was a challenge just to find them on television, if you were foolish enough to try.

Then there was the actual on-field product. As bad as the 2011 and 2012 teams were—and they were horrible—the next version was even worse. Bottoming out their major league roster and payroll, the Astros essentially began holding MLB auditions for minor leaguers, many of whom were not ready for the pressure or demands of the show.

By 2015 the initial false steps of the Astros' rebuild would be filed away and on the verge of being forgotten, as a young core began to carry the team and the front office started to get ahead of the game. In 2013 the Astros talked up a team that ended up losing a franchise-record 111 games.

"You take a step back, and you really realize just how special it is," said new manager Bo Porter, during his introductory press conference. "It's like I told Jeff and I told Jim: this is not a steppingstone for me. I'm not looking to build the Houston Astros up to a championship organization and then run off and go someplace else. I'm all in. They know that, and they're all with me."

Porter, who was hired on September 27, 2012, boldly spoke of setting high expectations and constantly inspiring his team through leadership and personal motivation. He sounded more like a preacher or football coach than the manager of a "Quadruple A" team that would soon fight just to win 51 games in a six-month season.

"The players that we've been able to acquire, they might not be known to the baseball community or they may not be household names," Porter said. "But when you look at the talent level and the projection of that talent level, we know what we have. It's just a matter of basically getting them to play to their potential."

A rising name in MLB, Porter had been the third-base coach for a Washington Nationals team that had won 98 games in 2012, eventually falling to the Cardinals in a National League Division Series finale. Washington had gone from a 69-win team in 2010 to one of the game's most-thrilling clubs in just two years. The energetic and charismatic Porter had connected with the Nationals' young players, and his ability to overcome a tough childhood had also led to an edge the Astros were looking for. If you were going to run out prospects and no-namers, you needed daily discipline.

"When you are born and raised in the community and the atmosphere in which I was born and raised in…the strong will survive—and that's probably putting it lightly," Porter said.

At the time, he was seen as a perfect fit for the new Astros. Luhnow referred to Porter as a manager who could last, and the organization believed that Porter could accelerate the team's growth on the field.

"Our staff is going to do a lot better job and I think that's where a lot of Bo's strengths come into play," Luhnow said. "No one's going to—I think discipline is going to be pretty good in the Bo Porter environment. Because he's going to have high expectations, he's going to be very clear about what he wants and how it needs to be done. And he's also going to be very proactive in disciplining players who aren't performing to his expectations. That's what we need. That's what a young team needs. It has to be done in a way where veterans can slide in there and also provide a little leadership and not feel like they're back in kindergarten. They need to feel like they're being treated like adults, as well."

Chemistry was one of the Astros' biggest assets during their championship run under A.J. Hinch. Winning fueled togetherness and sacrifice, which fueled more winning. By May 2013, though, the Astros' slow pace and constant losing was already beginning to wear on Porter. When asked about rebuilding, the first-year manager hired to guide the rebuild acted like he did not know the word existed. As for the Astros discarding almost all their remaining veterans and willingly giving MLB roster spots to minor league talent? "I've never used the word 'tryout,'" Porter said. "I don't know where that word came from. Can you rephrase the question?"

The theatrics started during spring training in Kissimmee, Florida, when a motivational spinwheel was placed inside the team's clubhouse and postgame mound celebrations saw the Astros high-fiving like a Little League squad. The show continued Opening Day, when Porter proudly displayed an orange "I'm All In" T-shirt for national TV cameras and his players dressed inside a revamped clubhouse that bore their new manager's own quotes on the walls, despite the fact Porter had yet to win a single big-league game.

The intentionally upbeat tone kept getting hammered, though. Being 20 games below .500 before June arrives takes a toll on everyone. "I didn't expect it to be easy," Porter said. "Anyone who would've expected it to be easy, I think they would've been naïve to the facts of everything that's going on. But I firmly believe that I'm up for the challenge. I firmly believe that our organization is up for the challenge. I believe in our vision. I believe in what it is we've all set out to do, and time will only tell."

Fan favorite Nolan Ryan, who helped guide the Astros to the 1986 National League Championship Series, acknowledged the obvious about rebuilding: it created an uncertain future. "Any time you see an organization go through a rebuilding process, it's painful," said Ryan, who was then serving in the Rangers' front office. "To have two 100-loss seasons [is] very painful for everybody associated with it. Hopefully, that will be the last year they have that."

The Astros' upcoming move to the American League—part of the sale process when Crane bought the team in 2011—was also conflicting and highly controversial to many longtime fans. Losing to win was one thing. But losing all the old traditions and changing everything, all while diving toward another 100-loss season?

"It's going to be different," said Ryan, who returned to the Astros' organization in 2014 as executive advisor. "I grew up with the Astros. The Astros, in my opinion, are a National League ball-club—that's the way I'll always view them. But from our perspective with the Rangers, to put somebody else in our time zone, it'll help us with some travel and also on our audience….When both teams are fighting for a [West] division title, it'll stimulate a lot of baseball interest in the state."

3

SAVING OUR POWDER

I have a strong faith that what it is we're doing, it's going to get better. I have a lot of confidence...in the players that we have in our organization. And I look at the big picture. I know a lot of times, the people outside of our clubhouse or the people outside of our circle, they're looking at the sample of the record, and that's pretty much all they see. I look at the players. I look at the overall objective of what it is we have to do as an organization.

—Former Astros manager Bo Porter

ONE OF HOUSTON'S greatest sports names knew exactly what the new Astros were: a work in progress. "I think that the fans understand that," Craig Biggio said. "I think the more honest you are, they understand it. It's just going to take us a little bit of time.... Baby steps, but we're getting there."

The major league product was altered piece by piece by piece. For Opening Day in 2012, Jordan Schafer led off for the Astros and Chris Johnson played third base. In 2013 Brett Wallace, Chris Carter, Carlos Peña, Justin Maxwell, Jason Castro, Matt Dominguez, Brandon Barnes, and Ronny Cedeño took the field with José Altuve, while Rick Ankiel pinch-hit.

The Astros' payroll had fallen to the $25 million range, which meant that the Yankees' Alex Rodriguez ($29 million) was making more in one season than the entire Houston team. "Spending money sometimes can actually be detrimental to your organization.

We don't consider that the objective," general manager Jeff Luh-now said. "How much money you spend is a result of what our strategy is, and how good we are at executing our strategy. Where that number ends up—whether it's 30 [million], 40, 50, or 100—that's not what's going to drive our decisions."

During the early years of the Astros' turnaround, spending money on the big-league product often did not make practical sense. A few million would not have made a real impact, especially for an organization that was deeply embracing analytics and build-ing off the foundation of the *Moneyball* era. It would have taken a sudden $100 million infusion to truly juice up the Lastros, and that route would have conflicted with their long-term plans. Lose now to win later. But when you win, keep winning and winning and winning.

While it was a simple baseball decision at the time, Lance Berk-man's choosing to play his final season with the 91-win Rangers in 2013—instead of re-signing with his old team, with which he had spent 12 seasons and was now set to lose 111 games—said every-thing about where the Astros' priorities were. They would spend real money...when the time was right.

"All of the formula is coming together, and we're saving our powder for when it'll have the most impact," said owner Jim Crane, who came close to purchasing the Rangers in 2010 before buying the Astros from Drayton McLane for $610 million. "If you talk to any baseball experts, we could've spent quite a bit more money and it may not have gotten us anywhere—it may [have] even set us back a little bit on chemistry."

Despite all the criticism of the Astros' miniscule 2013 payroll and the constant accusations of tanking, the organization was play-ing within MLB's rules and ultimately following the groundwork established by other franchises. No one had broken it down as far as the Astros. But they were far from the first team to lose big up front, then win bigger down the line.

"I do trust the organization," then MLB commissioner Bud Selig said. "Look, every organization goes through certain phases. They have chosen the path with some very qualified people. And the only way you can really build a solid organization, a solid team, is through a very productive farm system. And I think they're doing it the right way. There's no question in my mind."

Selig referenced the Atlanta Braves, offering a reminder that a team that made 14 consecutive playoff appearances from 1991 to 2005 (a strike wiped out the 1994 postseason) and won the 1995 World Series spent the latter half of the 1980s as one of the worst teams in pro sports. Atlanta lost and lost, then built one of the best and most consistent franchises in any sport during the last century.

"[The Astros are] getting good draft choices. They've drafted very well and wisely. And I think Houston fans have a lot to look forward to," Selig said. "If their rebuilding program is as good as I think it is and they think it is, they're going to create a lot more great memories."

Not in 2011–2013.

The Astros' first game of the 2013 season—a rebranded team, playing in a new league with a new manager—was their biggest and, in many ways, only highlight of the year. The 8–2 victory against the Texas Rangers at Minute Maid Park was also the only time the Astros were above .500 all season. They dropped their next six games and were 8–19 when May arrived. Even when they won seven of eight contests heading into June, they still were going nowhere and already starting to break apart. Porter's team was 33–61 at the All-Star break. Jason Castro was the club's only Midsummer Classic selection, not Altuve, and the main drama heading toward the non-waiver trade deadline was when the Astros would trade outspoken starting right-hander Bud Norris.

There was a fight between two pitchers, verbal backstabbing amongst the coaching staff, and an ever-growing list of disposable names: Trevor Crowe, Marc Krauss, Jake Elmore, Travis Blackley,

Paul Clemens, Chia-Jen Lo. But there were also prospects who would still be around in 2018 (Max Stassi) and a few key pieces of the Astros' 2017 world championship team, including Marwin González, who was limited to 72 games and only hit .221.

Carlos Peña, a respected 13-year veteran, had spent years playing for Joe Maddon with the rising Rays and was a key bat on a 2008 Tampa Bay team that advanced to the World Series. He had also played for Terry Francona in Boston and been on the *Moneyball* Oakland A's.

Peña would play 85 games for Bo Porter's Astros before being designated for assignment. A team that was on pace to break the MLB record for most losses in a season—held by the 1962 New York Mets, an expansion team that became loved for being so horrible—would be down to minor league callups and third-chance names by the end of the year. The Astros were hitting rock bottom in their rebuild and the big-league team was currently expendable during the grand experiment.

"This has been a very hard test for [Porter]," Peña said. "We have not played well, okay? And the times that we have, we haven't been able to materialize them into wins. So that's very tough for a manager to take. And I think he's done so gracefully, with a lot of strength, because he hasn't laid down. That is very hard to do because he's human, he's not a robot. He understands the inner strength that you must have to, despite the situation, come out with a positive outlook and attitude. It takes superhuman strength. The easy thing to do is to fold. But Bo doesn't do that."

Porter attempted to reach and inspire the new Astros. But there was already a growing feeling that, when the team did finally win, he would not be around to see the success. "People may think they have the answer today," said Porter, as the Astros were about to get swept at home by the Rangers in mid-May. "But, realistically, the answers to the questions in which many people want an answer today, you're not going to have a definitive answer until three or four years from now. The definitive answer will let you know whether or not the Houston Astros did the right thing. But what I will tell you, sitting here today, I firmly believe that we're doing the right thing."

As bad as the Astros were in 2012–2013, they were on to something—in some ways.

Robbie Grossman—who was a near-everyday player for the Minnesota Twins in 2017—was a classic early Astros project. A sixth-round pick in the 2008 draft, Grossman lacked power but gradually worked his way up through the minors. With the 2013 Astros, he suddenly became the team's starting center fielder just 21 games into the season. The traditional and accepted route was to gradually blend in prospects with proven, experienced veterans. The Astros were doing the exact opposite and made no apologies for it.

After making his debut in Houston against the Mariners, Grossman was then pushed onto two of baseball's biggest stages: Fenway Park and Yankee Stadium. The year prior, he had been in Double A. In 2013 he was suddenly being thrown "in the fire," as an Astros coach put it, at the sport's highest level. "I had many dreams of [Fenway] playing in my front yard as a kid," Grossman said. "It's just a surreal experience being here and actually being able to do it."

Then there was an early season 3–0 loss to the Mariners, which began the Astros' first road trip of the season. Despite entering Seattle with a 1–5 record and almost everyone in baseball knowing the Astros were destined for at least 100 defeats again, Porter pulled future slugger J.D. Martinez from the contest mid-game, then told the media to ask the young outfielder—who eventually received a $110 million contract with the Boston Red Sox in 2018—what had happened. "That was a manager's decision....I'm actually interested in what he's going to tell you," Porter said.

In the top of the fourth with one out, Martinez swung at the first pitch he saw and popped out to second. Martinez later acknowledged the problem was a hitting-related issue that had been discussed during a pregame batters' meeting. "From a baseball standpoint, I made a mistake [Monday]," an apologetic Martinez said. "I had a mental error going up to the plate. It was totally my fault. I understand everything Bo did taking me out. I hold nothing against him, because what I did was unacceptable. It was a mental mistake that will never happen again."

It was also a scene straight out of high school for a team that was still two seasons away from even contending for the playoffs.

The Astros were teaching—and messing up—on the fly during big-league games that counted. And some players they were trying to reach were openly rebelling. By 2017 defensive shifting would be widely accepted in MLB. The sight of Altuve playing second base in shallow right field would be commonplace. In May of 2013, several Astros players were still fighting the growing trend and blaming the analytics-based decision to move around position players for daily pitching woes.

"We're trying to do stuff with our defense right now, and it really worked against me," said No. 2 starter Lucas Harrell, after giving up seven hits and five runs in five innings during a 6–2 loss at Detroit that dropped the Astros to 10–30.

Harrell finished 2013 with a 6–17 record and 5.86 ERA.

Players were fighting the changes. But it was also easily understood why proud, competitive athletes were constantly feeling undercut by the team they played for.

During a four-game homestand in August against the Rangers—all Astros losses—veteran left-handed reliever Wesley Wright was traded to Tampa Bay for cash considerations. The Astros were 37–80 and only getting cheaper. Wright had been the longest-tenured member of the club and pitched in a team-high 77 games in 2012. The Astros' active payroll dropped to less than $13 million with Wright's departure. Veteran lefthander Erik Bedard ($1.1 million) was the only player left on the 25-man roster making more than $1 million.

Veteran Astros had joked all season with gallows humor. Who would be the next one to go? If you were making more than the league minimum, you were the next on the chopping block. Wright had joked after the non-waiver trade deadline that he was not sure how he had survived the constant departures during the rebuild. The youngest and worst team in baseball now employed 14 rookies.

"It's tough losing Wesley Wright, just because what it is he's meant to this organization," Porter said. "Throughout the entire time he's been here, since 2008, he's been great in the community, he's been a great teammate."

One of the biggest and most positive moves the Astros made all season was not a callup but an extension. In the middle of the worst year in team history, Luhnow locked down a player who would soon become the face of the franchise and the best overall hitter in the game. The Astros signed Altuve to a four-year extension on July 13, which included two affordable team options through 2019.

With the lowest active payroll in MLB, the extension represented the first major long-term commitment toward an Astros player in the Crane-Luhnow era. "We've got his face on the side of the stadium," Luhnow said. "He really has become the face of the franchise. And he is not only a good offensive player....He's been terrific in the community. So he really represents all the things that we want the Astros to represent."

As the Astros strengthened their commitment to Altuve, George Springer soared in the minors. One of former GM Ed Wade's lasting contributions to the rebuild hit .303 with 37 home runs, 108 RBIs, 106 runs, a 1.010 OPS, and 45 stolen bases combined at Double A and Triple A in 2013. In less than a year, Springer would be making his big-league debut. And when he arrived, he was not going back down. This was the real major league value that Luhnow had been working toward.

"I love playing the game. I love the fact that I'm in the lineup everyday," Springer said during his stay with the Double A Corpus

Christi Hooks. "It's just one of those things where I know there are thousands and thousands of other people who would love to be [on] this field, especially with this club. I go out and play hard. At the same time, I understand the only way to play this game is to have fun. The game's already hard enough. You just go out and have fun."

Springer had cleared every hurdle placed in his path, moving from short-season A ball to the best position player in the Texas League in less than two years. The 23-year-old center fielder had become the most electric athlete within an organization in clear need of major league buzz.

"The guy can do some amazing things," then Hooks hitting coach Tim Garland said. "He's a joy to watch, day-in and day-out. He's a hard worker, he plays the game hard. The sky's the limit with this young man. He does something every day that kind of like woos me. I'm just in amazement with how much ability this young man has. Obviously, he can hit the ball a country mile and he plays a wonderful, tremendous defense out there. He's got great instincts on the baseball field, and it's just a matter of time before this guy reaches Houston and gives the fans up there something to be excited about."

Carlos Correa was just as exciting and on an equally fast path to the majors. He would soon leap from Corpus Christi to Triple A Fresno and then the Astros in just one season. Correa was also noticeably mature by the end of his rookie season in the minors, bouncing from the Gulf Coast and Appalachian Leagues to winter ball in Puerto Rico. "I forget about everything else and I just focus on what I've got to do on the field," said Correa, as he played for Gigantes de Carolina in the winter of 2012. "It's really good to be here, and it's really enjoyable....This feels like baseball."

During the same season that Correa would make his MLB debut, Luhnow would make his first big deadline trade of 2015 by acquiring veteran lefthander Scott Kazmir from Oakland. At the end of 2012, while attempting to work his way back to the majors, Kazmir had crossed paths with Correa. "He has a good head on his shoulders," Kazmir said. "He's doing everything he's supposed to do. He's working hard every single day....You have to do that because baseball's a game based on failure."

As the franchise's young, promising names kept developing in the minors, the Astros' major league team only got worse. They returned from the break by losing 19 of 23, falling to an almost unthinkable 37–80 in mid-August. A home crowd of just 18,712 showed up to watch the Astros lose to Yu Darvish and the Rangers, and Houston finished its year by dropping 15 consecutive games, including Game 162 in 14 innings.

Houston endured three consecutive seasons with 100-plus losses, the last bottoming out at 51–111. Even the Astros' No. 1 pick in 2013, a reward for 107 defeats in 2012, ended up being a miss. Mark Appel only reached Triple A Fresno for the Astros before being traded.

The Astros had constructed a team, played baseball for six months, and finished 45 games out of first place in the AL West, all while further alienating their fan base. The rebuild was in progress but obviously still needed serious work and real major league names. It had almost always gone this way for the Astros—not annually being the worst team in baseball, but being unpredictable, coming up short, failing to deliver. That had often been the Astros' way since they began in 1962. Jeff Bagwell and Craig Biggio would soon reunite in the Baseball Hall of Fame. Nolan Ryan had been a part of some of the game's best teams in the 1980s. And from 1997 to 2005, the Astros made the playoffs six times, turning Houston into a baseball town.

But when they finally advanced to the World Series in 2005, they were swept by the Chicago White Sox. And a franchise that entered MLB as an expansion team—needing eight seasons just to break .500 and 19 to finally make the playoffs—had mostly disappointed a proud fan base that had become accustomed to heartbreak and painful letdowns.

As the Astros entered Porter's second year, the rebuild had already reached a dividing point. There was no set number of required wins in 2014. But frustrations that set in during 2013—the front office was not doing enough to support the big-league club; the MLB team was not playing up to its potential and properly developing young talent—were also not going away.

The Astros were a better team in 2014. Dexter Fowler and Scott Feldman were added. Dallas Keuchel went 12–9 with a 2.93 ERA, setting up his Cy Young year a season later. Altuve hit a league-leading .341 and racked up 225 hits. But they also started 10–24 and were 12 games under .500 entering July 1. The most important highlight of the season was Springer's MLB debut in April.

Criticism and controversy also continued to shadow the Astros. After taking Correa and Appel at No. 1 overall in back-to-back amateur drafts, the team failed to reach an agreement with 2014 first pick Brady Aiken, a high school lefthander. The Astros also did not sign fifth-rounder Jacob Nix. "Today, two young men should be one step closer to realizing their dreams of becoming major league ballplayers," MLB Players Association executive director Tony Clark said in a July 18, 2014, statement. "Because of the actions of the Houston Astros, they are not. The MLBPA, the players, and their advisers are exploring all legal options."

In a statement the same day, the Astros said their offer to Aiken was "extremely fair considering all the factors involved in this case." The statement added, "As always, we approached these negotiations in good faith and with the best interests of the Astros organization in mind, both short-term and long-term. Throughout this entire process, we have absolutely acted within Major League Baseball's rules and guidelines, which MLB has confirmed on numerous occasions."

A year later, Aiken had undergone Tommy John surgery—concerns about his elbow had led to a breakdown in contract negotiations—while the Astros had selected future starting third baseman

Alex Bregman out of Louisiana State University with the No. 2 over-all pick of 2015, which was compensation for not signing Aiken.

Correa also had season-ending surgery in June after breaking his right fibula. And while Appel struggled in the low-level minors—a promotion to Double A and a brief bullpen session at Minute Maid Park became a source of contention—Kris Bryant, the No. 2 over-all pick of 2013 and the player chosen by the Chicago Cubs after Appel, was lighting up the minors in 2014 and on his way toward being named the National League Rookie of the Year a year later.

Then there was the hacking. Two 2017 draft picks and $2 million were eventually awarded to the Astros after former St. Louis scout-ing director Chris Correa illegally accessed the Astros' "Ground Control" player-evaluation system. Even the Astros' secret inter-nal plans and discussions were being exposed. The hacking, which occurred during the early stages of the Astros' rebuild, resulted in a 46-month federal prison sentence for Correa.

On August 27, the Astros played to a home crowd of 14,791. Prospect Jon Singleton was hitting .185 but still receiving major league at-bats. Gregorio Petit was playing a position that future All-Star Carlos Correa would occupy a season later. Carlos Corpo-ran, Jesus Guzman, and Matt Dominguez were representing a team that was not even close to being a playoff squad and would not reach .500 without more major changes.

Porter was fired September 1. All the big talk at the start of the Astros' overhaul—self-help quotes, mirrors for personal reflection in players' lockers—was ringing hollow. After a simmering divide between the manager's side and the front office, Crane's franchise backed Luhnow and his vision. The Astros were suddenly in search of a calm but passionate leader who could unify the clubhouse and bring something to Minute Maid Park that had not been seen in a long time.

Winning.

4

THE UNDERDOG ALL YEAR

Being the first year here in Houston, and talking about this club from the beginning of February, I'm really proud of this group. We've earned every win we had this year....I felt like we came on to the scene with a little bit of surprise for a lot of people, not in our clubhouse but around baseball. As the story grew and we found ourselves in first place for the better part of five months, there was a storybook part of this. And the players embraced it, the coaches embraced it. We were loving every minute of it. And then things got a little heated and intense, a little hot.

—A.J. Hinch

IT HURT—BAD—when it was suddenly over.

A.J. Hinch was left with watery eyes. Young Astros hugged and consoled each other, knowing they had come so close, so soon, then suddenly let it all slip away. In the same year that Dallas Keuchel would win the American League Cy Young Award and become one of the best pitchers in baseball, the bearded lefthander would hold back tears as he embraced Colby Rasmus and let the emotion of 2015 wash over him.

"It's just tough, man," said Keuchel, his voice breaking. "It's tough."

It was also a total blast and the true beginning of a run that would end up with a World Series title just two years later.

The rebuilt Astros finally came to life in 2015. Much of what they accomplished in 2017 was set up by an unexpected run that blended Hinch's first season in orange and blue with the major league debuts of Carlos Correa and Lance McCullers Jr. Just two years after losing a franchise-record 111 games, the Astros were already a World Series contender—even if major league baseball was not ready for them to be so good, so fast.

"I think about it every day," Keuchel said. "I mean, my first year in 2012, and 2013, 100 losses. So that's something I don't forget, and that's something you'll never forget, just how bad it was and how quickly we've turned things around. Never want to go back there. So I'm always thankful every day I get to put this uniform on with the Astros on the front and enjoying winning."

The change began with youth, maturation, and leadership. It was driven by major league promotions, trades, signings, and waiver claims—general manager Jeff Luhnow proving that he knew exactly what he was doing. Evan Gattis, Will Harris, Hank Conger, Luke Gregerson, Pat Neshek, Luis Valbuena, and Rasmus would become Astros for the 2015 campaign. Alex Bregman would be drafted No. 2 overall. But no one made an impact like Hinch, who finally put winning at the forefront in Houston, blending modern analytics with old-school mental toughness. Hinch was a perfect fit the moment he began calling the shots.

"We've got to play 162. As much as that sounds like a cliché, the reality is at this level things can turn pretty quickly," Hinch said in December 2014, at MLB's annual winter meetings. "I do believe in the positive steps forward that this team saw last year....I will tell you that's still 20-plus games shy of what it's going to take to get into the playoffs. Certainly the emphasis has to be more about winning, more about propelling ourselves forward. Now, where those additions come from...this isn't a perfect science as to how to put it all together. I expect our team to come out and want to win every day. You only celebrate 70 wins so much. That type of attitude downstairs in the clubhouse—when we show up every night, we're going to put a team on the field we feel can beat the other that night."

As for the GM that Hinch would now be working with?

"People underestimate his desire to win—his desire to win and win for a long time," Hinch said. "Nobody likes to say 'rebuild.' Nobody wants to say 'remake.' Nobody wants to say 'revamp.' But getting this organization back to where we belong has been a long process. It's still going to take a lot more work. He never turns off. He is a continuous thinker. He's not afraid of challenge....What I found is he's pretty tireless in his pursuit to try to figure it out and figure it out quickly."

Luhnow was cerebral and highly driven. Hinch was just as driven—but calm and cool, even in the hottest moments. A Stanford-educated, first-year manager who seemed to just watch, observe, and stare, locked into a Zen-like trance. As the Astros' games only became more emotional and chaotic, Hinch only became cooler. But that was only part of his story.

"I go off with the best of them," said Hinch, who became the 18th manager in franchise history on September 29, 2014. The family that loved Hinch and the friends who really knew him could not believe he had not been shown blowing up on camera. All the television showed was a fit 41-year-old kneeling near the top step of the dugout for nine innings, surveying an unpredictable chess match that played out daily in ballparks across the country. But when the pieces suddenly fell apart or the plot evaporated with a single swing, Hinch felt the burning pain as much anyone in the stadium.

"Oh, I'm going, *Oh my God*," he said. "I have to go for a walk and get it out of my system. Behind the scenes, I've done a few things that I'm not the most proud of that players have seen. But that's the competitor in me, and it's okay for them to see that."

It was the real Hinch—a manager who could push, challenge and bark at his players, but also prided himself on building lasting personal relationships. The Astros needed heart. Hinch believed in humans. It was the vow he had made to himself when baseball came calling again with another shot at running a big-league club. I will be me and you will be you, Hinch had told and shown his team since spring training. But when we are on the field, we are all Astros.

"He just exudes confidence," McCullers said. "You can feel it coming from him. He loves his team, he trusts his team, and he'll run us out there against anyone, any day. When you can feel that— everyone can talk about it—but when you can feel that from a manager, it means a lot more to the guys and they play with that much more intensity, that much more heart. Because he's backing you up."

Hinch's combined 89–123 record during two abbreviated years in Arizona did not show it. But he did some good things from 2009 to 2010 with the Diamondbacks, while also making classic rookie mistakes. "I was very much fixated on what it looked like and what the perception was," Hinch said. "It" was everything. The team, the players, the clubhouse. The endless big picture of the season and the overwhelming minutiae that defines everyday life at the ballpark.

During his second run on the top step, Hinch started getting "it" right. He was himself while allowing the Astros to be exactly who they were. Silly, fun, and weird. Passionate, powerful, and erratic. The full arc of young, modern baseball at its brightest. But also the quieter world of veterans, backups, and castoffs, who also felt at home inside a sometimes college-like clubhouse.

"We have to understand societally where we are with how these players have grown up," Hinch said. "We have a ton of personality. And then I ride them pretty hard about the baseball....I have incredibly high standards for this team."

When third baseman Jed Lowrie was deciding whether he wanted to rejoin the Astros a second time, he met with Hinch before signing. Out of all the questions asked and inside baseball discussed, Lowrie had one main point he wanted to press with his potential new manager: are you going to micromanage everything or give the young guys a chance to actually prove they're pros? Lowrie soon got the answer he wanted and agreed to become an Astro again. "He's done a really good job of knowing when to say something and knowing when to back off," Lowrie said. "And that's the best quality a manager really can have, because you have all these dynamic personalities in the clubhouse."

The human side of the game did wonders for the chemistry of the team, clubhouse and front office. Bo Porter, the first manager of the Astros' new era, was a fierce proponent of new-age-speak and talking things into action. But his shorter-than-expected tenure was riddled with infighting and negativity, with insiders and outsiders eventually wondering why the organization had hired Porter in the first place. Too much meddling and friction, not enough trust. Hinch established an immediate rapport with Luhnow, whose relationship with Porter had deteriorated while the Astros' rebuild progressed.

"[Luhnow has] been terrific this year in terms of support, in terms of creative ideas, in terms of just being a sounding board for me about our team," Hinch said. "Yet he's kept his distance and allowed me to do my job, and I've appreciated that type of freedom."

Luhnow's second managerial hire had been one of his smartest moves since he started rebuilding the Astros. "I have no complaints," he said. "[Hinch] knows the game very well.…He asks for feedback. But I don't have a lot of feedback to give him, because he makes good decisions."

The freedom under Hinch increased as the Astros rose. They started 4–6, still playing to home crowds that struggled to break 20,000. But a 14–1 stretch followed, and the first buzz from Minute Maid Park in years didn't stop until a magical 2015 season finally did. Hinch's Astros reached 25–13 in mid-May, then 40–28 in mid-June. Collin McHugh started 9–3; Keuchel reached 11–3 before the All-Star break; and the May 18 debut of McCullers signaled the convergence of youth, potential, and power that would come to define the Astros during the next few years. This was what Jim Crane and Luhnow had been hoping for when they first started knocking it all down.

A team once mocked for its ridiculously cheap, nameless roster suddenly featured likable players who were becoming must-sees as the summer approached. In turn, the remade Astros restored Houston's pride and fans' belief in a baseball franchise. Altuve and Keuchel gave the Astros two All-Stars, marking the first time since 2004 the team had multiple starters in the Midsummer Classic. With the tease of a division race and the postseason becoming more real every day, Houston was returning to its status as a baseball town.

Even with a six-game losing streak in mid-July—preceded by a disabled-list stint for George Springer, who suffered a broken wrist after being hit by a pitch July 1 against Kansas City—and Mike Trout's Los Angeles Angels also rising in the AL West, the Astros were still ahead of schedule. By early August, they were 60–46 and held a four-game division lead. Few, if any teams, in the league were better than Hinch's when everything clicked.

"There's no doubt that our best is good enough," Hinch said. "We have the opportunity based on the first 100-plus games we've played. And we have the talent to make things interesting for us and have a special last couple months."

Keuchel carried the Astros all season. The crafty lefty was 3–0 in April, 4–1 in May, 4–1 again in August, and 4–2 in the regular season's final full month. At home, Keuchel was almost unhittable. The left-field corner at Minute Maid Park soon featured his name—fans dressed up in orange and proudly sported fake beards—as the seventh-round pick of the 2009 MLB amateur draft (Arkansas) went a sparkling 15–0 with a 1.46 ERA in downtown Houston, striking out 139 and walking just 28 in 129 1/3 home innings.

"The support has been great, not only for the corner but for the team as well, and that's been nice to see," Keuchel said.

The No. 1 overall pick of the 2012 MLB draft gave the Astros even more support. And by the time October rolled around, there was no doubt that Carlos Correa was born for baseball's biggest stage. "The moment's never too big for him," Hinch said. "National TV, pennant race, an archrival in state."

Correa debuted June 8 against the Chicago White Sox at U.S. Cellular Field, hitting sixth and going 1-for-4 with an RBI during a 3–1 defeat. The Astros' lineup that night: Springer, Jonathan Villar, José Altuve, Gattis, Chris Carter, Conger, Marwin González, and Jake Marisnick, with McCullers on the mound and Tony Sipp in relief. For the next 98 regular-season games, Correa would impress, wow, and astound. He led the way, instead of following. He fit and blended right in, while still being himself. He possessed power, speed, vision, and range, and literally seemed to improve every single day. And he was also playing shortstop as a 20-year-old for an unproven, untested team in the middle of a playoff race.

On September 26, Correa unleashed a two-homer, three-RBI game that cemented the arrival of a future star. Down 3–0 to the Rangers after the first half inning at Minute Maid Park, Correa ended up 3-for-4 and put his new team on his back for a 9–7 victory. There was a solo shot that blasted past the Crawford Boxes and disappeared into the glare of afternoon sunlight. There was a rocket that left the bat with the same sharp crack, then fired on a hard line over the left-field wall. There was also a walk and nine total bases during a game the Astros had to win just to stay alive in their division. "Showrrea" was dominating the sport at the same time that baseball was still figuring out just how good the No. 1 overall pick could be.

Correa's 21 homers had tied Lance Berkman's franchise rookie record and were the most by a shortstop in club history. With two outs, Correa was hitting .374 (49-for-131) with 11 home runs. And in 92 rookie games, he was batting .282, slugging .520, and had 22 doubles, 61 RBIs, and 12 stolen bases.

In late September with 35,736 buzzing fans and baseball roaring again in downtown Houston, Correa ripped a couple bombs to silence the Rangers. "You can't even describe it....When I'm running to first, I'm like, 'Let's go!'" Correa said. "You get pumped up, and the adrenaline starts running all over your body."

As Correa tried to put the magic into words inside the Astros' clubhouse, Craig Sager watched from about 10 feet behind. Sager was known on TV sets around the world and regularly interviewed the biggest names in the NBA. But the broadcaster—at the time battling acute myeloid leukemia at MD Anderson Cancer Center—listened intently to everything Correa said, then quietly walked up and shook his hand. Sager had been watching the Astros all year. After watching Correa play baseball in person, he just wanted to say hi.

The Astros had received an endless amount of criticism during the early years of their rebuild. Taking Correa at No. 1 was a franchise-changing move that paid dividends the moment he reached the show.

Correa hit five home runs in both June and July, six in August, and five again in September. By the end of his abbreviated rookie season, he would hit .279 with 22 homers, 22 doubles, 68 RBIs, 52 runs, 14 stolen bases and an .857 OPS in just 387 at-bats, earning the AL Rookie of the Year award.

In September, Correa calmly walked toward his locker postgame, answering a circle of cameras, reporters, and recorders with two words seldom heard by high-profile athletes in the Twitter age. "Hello, guys," said Correa, who made sure an orange Astros hat was fixed to his head before the questions rolled. He was friendly, engaging, and telegenic. He was also years beyond his age, as were many of the Astros' rising young stars.

Major league baseball's surprise team in 2015 exceled at fun with a capital *F*. Club Astros began as a minor postgame experiment during the Astros' first road trip. It became an all-out war of fog machines, strobe lights, and club music. DJ Springer dreamed up the beginnings of the routine. It reached a point where it was a downer when Club Astros wasn't hopping after a game's final out was gloved. "It's just become a part of who we are," said Springer, who remained close to his team during his time on the disabled list and had a signed blue cast to prove it.

Hinch formed deep bonds throughout the team. But one of his strongest was with Springer. They were like father and son, coach and player, brothers, and more. "George is as consistent as they come with how he attacks life. His energy's authentic. It's real," Hinch said. "There's no bravado or fakeness—this isn't for show. It's just his personality. He's very infectious....To show up and see him every day is one of the best parts of my day."

Springer was equally complimentary of his new teammate, praising Correa's maturity as a rookie. That was the thing about the Astros' young core: once they were united in the big leagues, they immediately meshed on the field and were just as tight off it. "[Correa] has been everything as advertised," Springer said. "For being 21, he's got incredible poise. The skill-set is there. He's only going to improve. His poise, his calmness has been the thing that's kind of impressed us all. There hasn't been a day where I can say, 'All right, hey, you know, slow yourself down.' He's been calm the whole time, and I think he was able to show everybody what he can do. And he's obviously only going to improve."

Correa, Altuve, Keuchel, McCullers, Gattis, and company made the Astros fun in 2015. So did the constant walkoff homers, sharpened defense, strengthened rotation, and improved bullpen. But the craziness started with Springer—the heart, blood, and soul of the new Astros—and there was no way he was going to give up his baseball life while his team was having the best time of theirs. "It's not just putting on a smile and acting like everything is okay," said Springer, whose energy outshined a stutter he had dealt with since childhood. "I truly believe that everything is okay."

Springer would command the Astros' oversized HDTV in the clubhouse, playing a college football video game against anyone who would sit next to him. An hour later, he would be pure electricity around the batting cage. When the Angels came to town, Springer's batting-practice act was characterized by the injured outfielder imitating other Astros—walking like a 1950s space robot, throwing his hat off, throwing someone's glove away, and joking with everyone in sight wearing orange.

"Hey, A.J.," Springer said to Hinch, who was quietly resting against a dugout rail at Minute Maid Park.

"Hey, George," the manager said.

"You look confident today," Springer said. "I can see it in your face."

"You guys wear on me," joked Hinch.

"Why?" Springer said.

"Because I get tired of carrying this team every day," Hinch said. Springer cracked up. Hinch grinned.

"I see!" Springer said. "The brains behind the operation!"

As the Astros approached a critical make-or-break point in their season, their looseness and honesty were benefits, not hindrances.

"We understand what's at stake and the gravity of it," Springer said. "But ultimately in the end, it's a game, and this game's already hard enough. You can't play it tight. You can't play it stressed out."

Hinch's team had started a surprising 15–7, then gone 16–13 in May. June was 15–14, though, and July saw the Astros as a .500 team engaged in an increasingly tight battle for the AL West. A year prior, the Astros had finished 70–92 and fired their manager in September. In 2015 the Astros had exceeded everyone's initial expectations—including their own—but were now entering the non-waiver trade deadline with a major decision to make. They were going to be buyers for the first time in a long time. But how deeply invested was the front office in the present, when everyone knew the Astros' long-term future was their biggest goal?

From 2011 through 2014, the Astros hoarded prospects and used every trick possible to save money. But in one week midway through an already surprising 2015 season, Luhnow shipped away prospects for Scott Kazmir, Carlos Gomez, and Mike Fiers, attempting to give the Astros a jolt that would last through October.

The rebuilt Astros were changing—for the better.

"They talk about high leverage for relievers. This is a high-leverage opportunity for our club," said Luhnow, after acquiring Kazmir from Oakland on July 23. "We're in a division with one other team that seems to be our biggest challenge to winning. We owe it to ourselves to take advantage of this."

A year that was supposed to be about playing .500 ball and the return of on-field respectability was now devoted to making the playoffs for the first time since the Astros' lone Word Series appearance in 2005. "That's what our fans want. They want us to win... and we're taking advantage of it," Luhnow said.

By winning so soon, the Astros decided to keep adding on in 2015. Luhnow had taken a long glance at Minute Maid Park's increasingly filled seats and decided the future was now. "It means we're serious about doing some damage this year and in the years to come," Luhnow said. "It's going be a fun next few years for the Astros, and hopefully, it starts a long string of postseason appearances this year."

The trade-deadline acquisitions energized the clubhouse but did not give the Astros the initial spark they had hoped for. Fiers threw a no-hitter August 21, striking out 10 on 134 pitches during the Astros' 3–0 victory against the Los Angeles Dodgers at Minute Maid Park. But Kazmir was just 2–6 with a 4.17 ERA in 73⅓ innings, while Gomez only hit .242 with four home runs, 13 RBIs, and a .670 OPS in 41 games. The lack of immediate on-field value ended up affecting the Astros' deadline decisions in 2016 and 2017.

But a run from August 21 to 26 also reminded fans why Houston's baseball team was becoming so addicting in 2015. The Astros swept a three-game home series against the Dodgers, then took two of three against New York at Yankee Stadium. The sweep of the Dodgers capped a 7–3 homestand, which was punctuated by a walkoff home run from catcher Jason Castro. After Castro lifted a 96-mph fastball into the first row of the Crawford Boxes, the childlike Astros bounced and danced around home plate. "This is the most fun, exciting times since I've been here as an Astro. This has been a great season so far, and we just continue to add to it," said Castro, who was drafted by the franchise in 2008 and had endured all the pain of the organization's lost years.

Doubt the Astros. Think it is over. A club that kept capturing come-from-behind wins would somehow discover another way to breathe new life into fans and the season. "Everyone feeds off of it, and that's what it is," Kazmir said. "It's almost like we have that feeling now when we get to the ninth inning, if we're in reach, we feel like we can pull it off. And that's the team that you want to be."

They were a team. They had chemistry and unity. They also had enough talent to consistently cover up their holes. But the ahead-of-schedule Astros weren't officially ready in 2015, and their failure against the in-state rival Texas Rangers was the strongest reminder why.

Longtime Astros fans initially hated the idea of switching leagues and throwing away old partnerships. But after a dreadful 2013 and 2014 in the American League, Hinch's first season illustrated the potential of the Astros' new home in the AL West. The West Coast road trips and late-night television games were always going to be a difficult transition. But the Astros and Rangers had developed a real rivalry in just three seasons, and the 2015 campaign brought the intensity to the main stage. The only problem: the Rangers owned the Astros in 2015 and 2016, and a 6–13 mark against Texas' other baseball team in Hinch's debut season undercut everything the rising Astros were attempting to accomplish.

In mid-September, the Astros dropped four consecutive games in Arlington, Texas. A three-game division lead at the beginning of the month had become a two-and-a-half-game deficit. With call-ups, additions, and unexpected success, Luhnow had done a lot with a limited payroll in 2015. But the Rangers almost doubled the Astros' on-field big-league investments, with Texas' biggest names—Prince Fielder, Adrian Beltre, Mike Napoli, Elvis Andrus, Shin-Soo Choo, Yu Darvish, Cole Hamels—all coming with hefty price tags. "Fielder and Beltre are swinging the bats good lately," Altuve said. "They have more than 10 years in the league. They know how it feels and they know what to do."

The Astros had been magic for most of 2015. But they were D.O.A. for four forgetful days at Globe Life Park, beaten by a combined 33–13 and swept by a bigger, badder, better team. September was supposed to test the young Astros. Through 17 days, it had wrecked them. They had gone 4–11 during their most important month of the season, with arms dropping and bats falling asleep at the worst possible time. "The bottom line is we just got outplayed," Hinch said. "They found different ways to win games and executed pretty flawlessly."

Hours before the first pitch of the series finale, though, Hinch was as calm as ever. The first-year Astros manager even joked about whether he needed to put on an "angry" face before he went on camera inside the dugout, deflating the rising pressure with smooth wisdom. "Haven't we been the underdog all year?" he said. "From April on, we've been asked about—with a little bit of curiosity—how we're doing it. And for five months straight, we've answered the question the same way, which is we believe in ourselves, and we're going to play the game and see what happens."

The slide hurt the Astros. But their resilience kept coming through, and they had two weeks left to save a season that began with so much promise. "It'd be hard to say anybody in this room thought we were going to be in this position to begin with. And definitely people writing with their pens didn't think so," Rasmus said. "We're in a good spot. We've still got a long ways to go."

On September 25, Hinch's team was 80–74 and had dropped three straight at home. With their season on the line, they finally showed some life against the Rangers, taking two of three at Minute Maid Park. Staring at a six-game road trip to close out 2015, the Astros' clubhouse whiteboard said it all. Large letters were written in all caps, making sure no one missed the message: BRING PASSPORT. That is how the Astros were thinking, already believing they were going to the playoffs and preparing for a possible American League Division Series appearance in Toronto.

A manager who started talking about winning from the beginning had kept the Astros in the playoff picture for almost six full months. Hinch, who would finish second in AL Manager of the Year voting to the Rangers' Jeff Banister, had been the perfect voice for the Astros during his first year on the job. "[Hinch is] very open with a lot of the guys," Keuchel said. "He's a former catcher. I know a lot of managers have been former catchers, but his communication to us, he really doesn't hold anything back. I think that's what separates him from everybody else that we've had. Very open door. First day of spring training, it was calling me in. Just talked for like 10, 15 minutes about what the schedule's going to be like in spring training. And that's really never, at least in my view, it's never happened before....And it's been that way ever since. So if you need to go into his office and talk to him, he's there, and he just lets us play."

Hinch let the young Astros be themselves. Rookies dressed up as comic-book superheroes for a cross-country flight—Correa as Wonder Woman, McCullers as Batgirl, Preston Tucker as Bamm-Bamm—and a thrilling young team found its rhythm again.

"You guys like entertaining baseball?" asked a smiling Hinch, after the team that just would not go away guaranteed its first winning season since 2008.

Game 156 solely belonged to Keuchel. The lefty was cruel, filthy, and nasty in the best possible way during what was, at that point, the biggest game of his career. He threw seven innings of two-hit, one-run, 10-strikeout ball, powering closer toward a Cy Young Award. "It'd be nice to have some hardware," Keuchel said. "But I'd rather have a big fat ring."

In 2017 the Astros' first-ever world championship came down to Game 7 of the World Series, and reaching that final stage required two victories in AL Championship Series elimination games. In 2015 the season that began April 6 with a 2–0 victory against Cleveland in downtown Houston needed all 162 contests for a conclusion.

"Sunday's the most important game of the year," said Hinch, after the Astros won for the sixth time in seven games and approached Game 162.

5

WE'RE A [FREAKING] PLAYOFF TEAM!

It's very tough. There's not a man in that room who wanted the season to end. There's going to be 29 teams that go through what we're going through today. There's going to be one champion. So it hurts. It hurts to know that we put everything that we could into this season and [have] it end abruptly. Seasons like this end really quickly, and you're never ready for it.

—A.J. Hinch

TWO DAYS AFTER destroying the Arizona Diamondbacks 21–5 at Chase Field with Dallas Keuchel recording his 20th win of the season, the division title, the final American League wild-card spot, and hosting the wild-card game, among other possibilities, were all very much alive for the 2015 Astros.

"It's a blast. We've played [161] games, and we're right in the thick of things. How can you not have fun with it?" manager A.J. Hinch said.

They fell in Game 162 and the Texas Rangers won, but it ultimately didn't matter. The Los Angeles Angels also lost, which helped send the Astros to New York for a wild-card matchup at Yankee Stadium.

Cue the first postseason celebration in a decade. Considering that this one was for a team that wasn't even supposed to sniff the playoffs, the Astros went all-in the moment they knew their season was still alive. Shouts and screams inside a tarped-off, cramped clubhouse. Bass going boom, boom, boom as Club Astros kicked in again. Two years after losing 111 games, the 86–76 Astros were a playoff team—and a team that fans had already fallen in love with.

Hinch suddenly called the room to attention and brought silence. He had been fired by the opposing team five years ago. Now he was one of the best young managers in the game and had a team that was just beginning its ascension.

"When we got together in February...nobody outside this clubhouse thought we had a chance," said Hinch, engulfed by the drenched, New York–bound Astros. "You can say a lot of things about this team, right? One thing that they're going to say forever: we're a [freaking] playoff team!"

The spraying resumed and Club Astros was cranked back up to full blast.

"The [fans] have been through a lot. We've been through a lot," general manager Jeff Luhnow said. "This is an organizational effort from top to bottom, and I couldn't be happier."

When Hinch first interviewed with a rebuilding club, he was asked why he wanted to manage the Astros. Hinch gave an answer that was impossible during the 100-loss seasons: he wanted to feel champagne in his eyes. The Astros had delivered in year one, and their manager had been the perfect man for the job.

"The words can't describe it," Keuchel said. "I've never been on a playoff team before, so this is my first time celebrating like this. I wouldn't trade it for anything."

Colby Rasmus was also almost speechless. Then he took his shirt off, put on thick goggles, and became one of the many lives of the clubhouse party, double-fisting a celebration that was tied to a February 20 spring-training start in Kissimmee, Florida. "To put it into words is crazy," Rasmus said. "Poppin' bottles is easier."

Craig Biggio had made the Baseball Hall of Fame in January. Longtime Astros voices Milo Hamilton and Gene Elston had passed within 12 days of each other in September. It had been a long, pivotal year for the Astros, who had brought real baseball back to Houston and were getting hot again, just in time for the heat of October.

"Why not the World Series?" Hinch said. "Why don't we just go all the way to the World Series?"

The moment they arrived in the playoffs, it started to feel like they could. On October 6, the Astros blanked the Yankees 3–0 in New York. Keuchel added to his Cy Young–caliber 2015 season by throwing six innings of shutout ball at Yankee Stadium, striking out seven and only allowing three hits on 87 pitches. "Felt like playoff baseball. It's hard not to get up for a game like this. And if I had a chance to take the ball in the wild-card game, I didn't want to let my teammates down," Keuchel said. "I've worked so hard the last four years in the big leagues, especially with rebuilding with our team. I knew if we had a shot, I was going to give everything I possibly could.…Never would imagine that I would have pitched that well or we would have played that well in Yankee Stadium on that big of a stage. But that's what we've been doing all year. Nobody really gave us anything at the start of the year. And I don't think anybody gave us a shot at the end of the year."

Carlos Gomez and Rasmus went deep, while the Astros' bullpen (Tony Sipp, Will Harris, Luke Gregerson) shut down New York. The energetic Astros had regained their buzz just in time for the postseason, and they celebrated again as the AL Division Series awaited. Baseball's surprise team had suddenly ended the Yankees' season. "It's really disappointing. It's hard," New York manager Joe Girardi said. "You know, seasons end abruptly, and it's very difficult. This is a club that fought all year long, and there's a lot of character in that room and this hurts. And we just didn't get it done."

Few gave the Astros a shot against the Royals, especially with the first two games in Kansas City at Kauffman Stadium. But both teams were evenly matched between the lines, and the Astros were only getting stronger in October. "There's a lot of similarities," Royals manager Ned Yost said. "They're both young clubs. They both play with a lot of passion, a lot of energy. It looks to me like their chemistry is outstanding. I think A.J. Hinch has done a great job with that team in molding them and allowing them to be who they are and letting them use their best assets—their energy, their passion, their athleticism—to be successful."

The best regular-season team in the AL fell 5–2 to the Astros in Game 1 of the ALDS. Collin McHugh followed Keuchel's wild-card victory with six innings of two-run ball, and the Astros once again proved that they belonged among baseball's elite in 2015. "We know the talent we have in the clubhouse. We know the makeup of the group of guys we have, and we've believed in our-selves all year," McHugh said. "A.J., from day one, said we've heard a lot of talk about rebuilding and getting prepared the last couple years, but this is the year we're going to hear 'win' a lot more. For us, we kind of took it to heart. From the get-go, from the jump, we believed we had a good club and could compete with anybody."

The Royals needed a tight 5–4 victory in Game 2 just to break even as the series headed to Minute Maid Park. The Astros had been a different team in Houston, posting a 53–28 record in their own ballpark, compared to a 33–48 mark on the road. With Games 3 and 4 of the five-game series at Minute Maid Park, a playoff run that had already seen the Astros bounce from Arizona to New York to Kansas City in five days was on the verge of turning in Houston's favor. "I'm happy that we're going home. I know the Houston fans are ready for us to come home," Hinch said. "We've got home-field advantage for the rest of this series. We got to take care of business in our own backyard."

Thanks to unpredictable slugger Chris Carter, the Astros took a 2–1 series lead and were staring at two closeout games. An early part of the rebuild, Carter had hit just .223, .227, and .199 during three seasons with the team. But he also clubbed 37 home runs in 2014 and had powered through stretches when he was one of the most dangerous long-ball hitters in the big leagues. In Game 3, Carter was perfect at the plate: 3-for-3 with a double, home run, and two runs. An experiment the Astros had stuck with since 2013—huge home runs and random power versus empty swings and a ton of strikeouts—paid off big on October 11, 2015.

"He's hung in all year. It hasn't been an easy year for him. It's still been a relatively productive year for him. This guy's continued to hit homers and maintained his composure," Hinch said. "Some of his stoic behavior throws some people off—that maybe he's not internalizing it enough. But behind the scenes we get to see it, and to see him come up big in the biggest moments is really gratifying because we know how much work he's put in, we know how much he cares. We know the impact. I've sat in this seat and talked about how he can change the game....It doesn't surprise us that he has that kind of impact. I think for him to hang in there mentally and go through the struggles that he did and come out, as hot as he's been in the playoffs, is awesome."

The Astros turned a 1–0 fifth-inning deficit into a 4–2 win, sending 42,674 fans into an ear-piercing frenzy. Carter was hitting .455 (5-for-11) in the playoffs, and the Astros were just one victory away from the AL Championship Series. The team had dealt with criticism of Carter for three strikeout-prone seasons. In Game 3, he had his squad's back. "It means a lot to me to have my organization behind me like this. I struggled early in the season every year....It's nice to have that feeling that they have confidence in me, that I'll still come around and come through," Carter said.

The Astros would spend the next two years getting over Game 4.

It was all there, and it was all happening, so darn loud you could feel the sound shake your pounding heart. Carlos Correa went deep twice. "Altuve! Altuve! Altuve!" for the Astros' All-Star second baseman. Just six more outs. Then, suddenly, somehow, it all fell apart. The Astros' 6–2 lead in the eighth inning became silence, more silence, and then just pain.

"It felt like we were going to celebrate," Evan Gattis said.

They never did.

The never-say-die Royals scored five runs in the top of the eighth as the Astros' bullpen fell apart, added two more runs in the ninth, and brought the worst memories of scarred Houston sports fans—collapse, heartbreak, shocking and sudden letdowns—back to life.

"They never tried to come out of their shoes and try to change the score with one swing. So credit to them for their approach," Hinch said. "Obviously, to get six base runners on in a row, that's good team offense, which we have seen out of them for a lot of games. Not only in this series, but as you study them and see how they're successful, it's usually involving quality at-bats, and they executed them."

Harris gave way to Sipp, who gave way to Gregerson. Add in a Correa error, and the Astros simply fell apart after a season devoted to staying together and rising above.

"It's tough to look these guys in the eyes," Harris said.

The Royals' season-changing eighth: 53 pitches, 11 batters, five runs, five hits, two walks, one error, one stolen base, two pinch-runners, three Astros pitchers…and one huge Kansas City win. "The eighth clearly wasn't a good inning," Hinch said. "They put together some good at-bats. They put, what, five or six singles in a row. Had the ground ball up the middle. They just never quit. They put together really good at-bats, and we couldn't get the inning to end in any way."

"The thing about this club is that they don't quit," said Yost. "They don't. And after giving up three runs there in the bottom of the seventh, they came in on fire. Again, like they do. 'Come on, let's go, good at-bats, let's start it moving. On base, on base, on base, let's go, boys. Let's get it going.' That was an unbelievable inning. I think we ended up seeing like 53 pitches in the eighth inning. I mean, that just shows you the quality at-bats that we had, at-bat after at-bat after at-bat. So it was a great inning right there."

Kansas City first baseman Eric Hosmer, who went 2-for-5 with a home run and three RBIs, said, "We always feel that we're still in games and we still have a chance. You look at the beginning of that inning there, and [Alex] Rios starts it off, and then we follow up by another hit and we hit one out of the park or we get a double, we're right back in the game. So that's the mentality for this whole entire team. It's never quit, and the character we showed today, that's what a championship ballclub does."

The 2015 Royals sounded and played like the 2017 Astros. Which meant that a series-deciding Game 5 back in Kansas City was already feeling like just a formality. Beyond a stadium of blue there were trees with changing colors, as the last life of summer faded into bright orange. And on a field of green there was a baseball team wearing new "Take October" sweatshirts on a crisp fall day. The Astros did not just go away.

Marwin González wore a Looney Tunes T-shirt. Jonathan Villar tiptoed as he danced. Carter launched a 430-foot batting-practice shot just below the peak of Kauffman Stadium's crown. A brutal Game 4 killed the Astros. But they still had one more chance in Kansas City to keep 2015 alive.

"One thing that's been very consistent throughout the year is our ability to turn the page and wash off any of the stink of things that don't go our way," Hinch said. "So I knew that the flight would be that way. We showed up, got to our hotels, woke up this morning, the sun came out, beautiful day in Kansas City, and we'll be ready to play. The mood is great. We have played 167 games to get to this point, we have won a lot of them. We have a big one tomorrow. Everybody knows that, and our guys are ready. So they're very upbeat."

Luhnow was also optimistic. But the GM was still stomaching the fall of Game 4. He had watched the Astros rise from 55–107 to

86–76 in four seasons. Which meant he felt the pain of the eighth inning as much as anyone inside Minute Maid Park or watching the collapse on TV. "Being six outs away from the ALCS and having it slip away...that was hard to be a part of," Luhnow said.

After eight-plus months of living the sport and thousands of decisions for a few extra wins, there finally would be a finale. Someone's year was going to end. Someone was also going to stay alive, watching the colors continue to change as the rest of October played out.

"Game 5, season on the line, backs against the wall," Hinch said. "All that stuff makes it so much more intense and so much more enjoyable....If you had given me the opportunity to sign up for this in February, I would have taken it. But the fact that it's a reality makes it one of the best days of the year."

Hinch gave the ball to McHugh, a 19-game winner. The Astros took a 2–0 lead in the second inning after Luis Valbuena lifted a 94-mph Johnny Cueto fastball to right field. But the Astros ended up with only two hits, a recharged Kansas City club came through with eight, and it ended up 7–2 Royals in a stinging season-ender for Hinch's team. There was no revival or new life. After all the magic in 2015, Kansas City was moving on to much bigger things, while the Astros' season suddenly ended. Game 5 finished it, but Game 4 was the real divide.

"I think in time, time heals all wounds," Hinch said. "And we'll be able to reflect back on a lot of things that we learned about ourselves, we learned about our team. And a lot of good's going to come out of it. It doesn't feel like it right now. I got a lot of heartbroken guys in that clubhouse who really believed that we could continue on. But for the group of players that this was their first time in the playoffs, for me as a manager, first time in the playoffs, I'm proud of how we handled ourselves. I'm proud of how we responded to the challenge of a wild-card game, how we responded to the challenge of playing the defending American League champions, and how we gutted it out to the bitter end."

The Astros were back, and fans believed again. But for all the hope and pride that 2015 represented, the team's shortcomings were also a reminder of the work and distance that still remained. The young talent was obvious. An annual World Series contender could be built around George Springer, Altuve, and Correa. Holes had to be filled, and a few proven veteran names were still needed, though, and the rebuilt Astros were going to have to start operating like a big-money, big-market team if they truly wanted to be the final club standing when the playoffs were complete.

"There's still a commitment to winning, very much so," Luhnow said. "If that involves increasing resources even more, Jim [Crane] has assured me that the ownership group is behind us."

Money was not the only answer. But in modern baseball, it was normally part of the solution. Kansas City added Cueto and eventually ended up as World Series champions. The Texas Rangers ended up winning the AL West with Cole Hamels. The Chicago Cubs had collected young talent comparable to the Astros', but had also spent big money to fill in gaps and move their rebuild forward.

There would come a time in the near future when the Astros had to back Altuve, Springer, Correa, and Keuchel with proven, World Series–caliber names. As 2015 moved toward 2016, the Astros' general manager hinted at the changes still to come for Houston's baseball team.

"We're going to be able to drive revenues through attendance and a TV deal that's now in place and be able to keep our players," Luhnow said. "We're not ever going to have the payroll of the Yankees, the Red Sox, or the Cubs. But we should be able to keep [our] players. And if we're smart about how we make decisions, compete consistently."

The rebuild was entering the next stage.

6

GETTING INTO OUR WINDOW

We want to bring a winner here—a perennial winner. We want to bring a championship here....This city is aligned with what we're doing, and we feel that energy when [the stadium] fills up.

—A.J. Hinch

IT WAS SUPPOSED to be the year that they truly leapt forward.

A deeper, stronger roster. Further into the playoffs. Freely talking of the World Series and unafraid of the season-long pressure that came with all the chatter.

"It doesn't automatically get better because the calendar turns and we've gotten older and matured over the course of the season," A.J. Hinch said at the 2015 winter meetings. "We're not going to sneak up on anybody. I can't play the disrespect card, so to speak, of being a team that's not expected to win. I'm sure we're going to have some expectations on us. So our players will really like that. We had all year last year where there were continual questions on how good we were going to be, and that's going to be from the onset this year. And I welcome it. Our guys didn't get too high or too low last year based on the expectations. So I would expect our focus to be on the field, but it will be a little bit different in spring when teams are looking for Dallas Keuchel coming off a Cy Young season, and Carlos Correa now getting a full season in. With heightened expectations comes a lot more attention."

The 2016 season became a step backward for the Astros. And a reminder that a rebuilt franchise could not simply rely on young talent alone.

They added a closer, a prized international free agent, and another No. 1 overall pick to the big-league diamond. They again spent time as one of the best and hottest teams in baseball. But by the time their 2016 campaign was complete, the 84–78 Astros were two wins off their magical 2015 mark, only good enough for third place in the American League West, and still could not stand up against the Texas Rangers. By the end of a solid but ultimately disappointing season, Colby Rasmus was on his way out of town, Carlos Gomez would be gone, Jason Castro and Luis Valbuena had played their final games in Houston, and Alex Bregman and Yuli Gurriel were on the rise.

The 2015 season was supposed to set up another surge forward in 2016. But the 2016 season eventually set up 2017, shining a light through the Astros and displaying the holes the team could no longer afford to cover up.

Of course, it all began easy, loose, and free. Baseball's surprise team in 2015 returned to spring training in Kissimmee, Florida, for the final time. And when the highly energetic Astros arrived, they buzzed from the start and acted like their collapse in Game 4 of the ALDS against the eventual World Series champion Kansas City Royals had never even happened. Confidence, swagger, buzz—that is how the 2016 Astros began.

Correa was wrapped in a red No. 13 James Harden Houston Rockets jersey, shooting around the world as the basket kept rattling and the ball continued to find the bottom of the net. George Springer sat atop a nearby wall, a shining blue Houston Texans helmet strapped to his chin and a colored visor obscuring his young face. A.J. Hinch, calm and cool as always, stood in the middle of it all, surrounded by his entire team as a Sunday morning at Osceola

County Stadium was devoted to a high school–like basketball shootout of epic proportions.

"Sometimes you can't map it out any better than a couple of buzzer-beaters," said Hinch, on the same day the NCAA bracketed 68 men's basketball teams for March Madness.

The charm and perfectly carefree attitude were still there. But layered within the swagger was the growing realization that 2016 was going to be different for the Astros. For the first time since 2006, real expectations—both external and internal—had arrived. Suddenly reaching the ALDS meant that the ALCS (or the World Series) was obviously the next step. And the feel-good story of 2015—baseball returning in downtown Houston; the once-horrible Lastros actually worth watching and paying for again—now came with a new script.

"I get the stress that comes with a season in general, let alone a season with high expectations," Hinch said. But did his team? And could newly acquired closer Ken Giles, sent to Houston in a December 12 multiplayer package deal, consistently close down the ninth? Would Keuchel, the reigning AL Cy Young Award winner, return to earth? Was Rasmus really worth $15.8 million, even if it was just for one year?

Giles represented another step forward for the Astros. In 2013 the accepted joke was that the Astros did not need a closer, since they were not concerned with actually winning games. Then it was by committee and non-typical veterans filling in on a rotating cycle. The hot hand got the ball. With Giles, the Astros added a hard-throwing right-hander on the rise. They also did it on their terms, acquiring him from a rebuilding Philadelphia team and sending disappointing 2013 No. 1 pick Mark Appel—out of baseball by the spring of 2018—to the Phillies, in addition to other names.

Popping the mitt was normal to Giles. He could hit 100 mph and prided himself on his inner fire. "I knew I had a gift, and I decided to take advantage of it," said Giles, who had struck out

151 in 115²/₃ innings and held a 1.56 ERA before joining the Astros. The 6′2″, 205-pounder from Albuquerque, New Mexico, embraced being different. He was not squeezed from youth straight through a smooth, safe baseball pipeline. Giles played the sport for a living. But he also knew that life was about much more than just the game. "Life isn't always about unicorns and all these positive things," Giles said. "A lot of people think that everything should just be given to you. Especially the kids now, they all expect things to be given to them. And that's really not [it]. When they grow up, they're in for a world of hurt."

The Astros swore they were ready for the next big step. But when the season began, they started 2–4, then hit 4–8 and 7–17. And they never really recovered.

"A lot of people are saying that we can win the World Series and all this stuff," José Altuve said. "Inside the clubhouse, we know that we can go out there and win the World Series. But you don't want to think too much about that—it's a long season."

It only got longer and tougher. The Astros hit 17–28 on May 22 after being swept by the Rangers at Minute Maid Park. Keuchel struggled in April then hit a wall in May, going 1–3 with a 6.63 ERA. The team that had stunned major league baseball in 2015 and spent the following spring training pumping its World Series chest had started a new season by pressing too hard, trying to individually do too much, and falling face-first. "It sucks....We know what's going on. We've got to find a way to find solutions," said Hinch, after another home loss.

General manager Jeff Luhnow was already attempting to figure out just what it would take to make the Astros relevant in October. "As long as no one runs away with it and we're back to .500 by mid-June, we should be in pretty good shape," he said.

A rotation that had become overly dependent on its top two starters was unpredictable by May, with Collin McHugh and Keuchel struggling. Defense and base running also held back the team, which was either too tight or too loose during the early part of 2016. Evan Gattis, Preston Tucker, Marwin González, Castro, Gomez, and Valbuena were among the many Astros searching for their stroke. Almost the entire team was off target. "We need to make some improvements," Luhnow said. "And it's not waiting for someone to come around. It's everybody doing their part and everybody chipping in."

On May 22, the Astros were the fourth-worst team in baseball and last in the AL West, 10 games out of first place. Only one hitter on the roster was batting above .254. The 2016 Astros were still dealing with the holes from 2015 and didn't have the buffer of a hot start. Could they turn their own season around? Did they have the internal leadership to call themselves out? Those had already become critical questions by late May, with their once-promising season on the line.

Hinch had made lineup adjustments and minor changes. But the next step had to come from the team being paid to play, and the Astros struggled to find veteran voices that could alter the tone. The team's chemistry was still strong. But a 2015 club that had guided itself by committee—proudly welcoming all kinds, embracing both young stars and veteran castoffs—needed some direct old-school guidance.

"Nobody questions leadership when you're winning baseball games," McHugh said. "Nobody talks about who's going to step up and be the person when somebody's stepping up every night." The right-hander added, "I want to be honest, and I want to be open. But I can't point to anything in the clubhouse that is hurting us....We keep each other real loose. But at the same time...we do police each other."

Rasmus believed the Astros initially felt the pressure of their own heightened expectations, then tried too hard after a disappointing start. But in recent weeks, the club was simply losing the "game within a game," with a single strike, out, or missed opportunity dictating the daily outcome. "Do I start yelling at younger guys for taking a pitch that's this far off the plate and they're rung up on it?" Rasmus asked. "How am I doing them a service? Because we're taught not to swing at those pitches....That's kind of the double-edged sword we're at right now in the season."

Also, just because you scream does not mean it is going to make a difference. "I was on the Blue Jays," Rasmus said. "We had José Bautista and Mark Buehrle. And they came in and did it, and it didn't help nothing. We still ended up 15 [games] out."

It took until May 24 for the 2015 Astros to show themselves in 2016. Hinch's team won eight of nine games, ignited by a 3–2 victory against the Baltimore Orioles in 13 innings at Minute Maid Park. And on June 22, after a 20–8 run, they pushed above .500 for the first time since Opening Day, finally beginning to look like the team they were supposed to be.

Hinch worked in new young names, bumped Altuve out of the leadoff spot, and moved his bullpen arms around. Just as importantly, the Astros' second-year manager publicly remained calm and always backed his players when the microphones and cameras were on. He would privately challenge his team when needed. But Hinch constantly kept the 162-game grind in mind, focusing on the light instead of the darkness.

"One of the most important things is, he understands how hard it is to play this game....You're not trying to fail—there's no intent to fail," Springer said. "He understands that in order to have success in this game, you have to fail. And you're going to fail more times than you have success."

The Astros balanced those two outcomes constantly in 2016. Hinch knew better than anyone how damaging April was to his team. But his daily approach remained the same, and the man who emphasized the importance of the full 162 in 2015—which had paid off in game 162—knew that he could not suddenly change his outlook just because a team loaded with expectations had started a new season backward. "I'm pretty competitive behind the scenes," Hinch said. "I may not be as even-keeled as people like to see on TV or...in front of the media. I don't like losing. But the record over the course of the season is what I'm more fixated on, not necessarily the first six weeks."

Altuve was the Astros' lone constant. He hit .305 in April, .345 in May, rose to .420 in June, and batted .354 in July. His power was also rising. After hitting seven homers or fewer during his initial four major league seasons, the second baseman clubbed six in April while the 2016 Astros slumped through the first month of the season. Nationally, Altuve was still being underestimated and taken for granted. But locally, he was beginning to place himself among Houston's biggest sports stars, sharing the same mantel as Texans defensive end J.J. Watt and the Rockets' Harden.

Smoothing out his stroke and swinging at fewer pitches—including fewer outside of the zone—Altuve was becoming a more disciplined and powerful hitter with each passing month, driving the ball to all fields and attacking pitchers with pre- and in-game preparation, not just pure natural instinct. "What we're seeing is a more complete hitter who is maturing in front of our eyes," Hinch said, "who we thought was already mature, despite the really unnecessary stereotypes that come with being a smaller player."

During the Astros' 111-loss season in 2013, Altuve batted .283, struck out a career-high 85 times, and only posted a .316 on-base percentage. He also led the American League in times caught stealing (13) and posted a meager .678 on-base plus slugging percentage. Three years later, Altuve had become one of the best overall hitters in the game and still hadn't reached his peak at the plate. "He got up here at such a young age, and he got some success. He's an exciting player, he got a lot of hits, yet he was an unfinished product," Hinch said. "That's difficult to tell someone when they're having as much early career success as they've had...and there were still ways for him to get better."

The Astros' coaches aided Altuve in the batter's box and with the glove. But the real surge came from within. Driving the ball with runners on base, unleashing opposite-field power and turning his defense into an asset—areas where Altuve was knocked in his early twenties—had become some of his greatest strengths in 2016. Even a disappointing start for his team could not hold him back. "It's fun to watch someone so hungry be great and not just be content being good," Hinch said.

After their 17–28 start, the Astros reached 43–37 on July 1. It was not a coincidence that Altuve, Springer, and Correa had finally synced up together. Correa had been off during the season's initial two months, being overly patient at the plate and only hitting .239 in May. Springer had been on and off thus far in 2016. But the trio all clicked in June, and the Astros rolled off an 18–8 month, following the lead of their three young stars. For a time, Houston was again the hottest team in the sport.

Altuve produced a 1.112 OPS in June and was rewarded with AL Player of the Month. Correa also had his best month of the season: .303 average, 1.024 OPS, five home runs, and 22 RBIs. Springer only hit .202, but he blasted five long balls, had 15 RBIs, walked 18 times, recorded 21 runs, and made a series of circus-like catches in the outfield, pushing himself into All-Star contention. "When you have one good player, that player can help you win a ballgame," Luhnow said. "When you have two or three good players, it can help you have a good month and a good year and a good run into the postseason."

But the Astros still did not have a complete team that was strong enough to discover an answer for the Rangers. A year later, the Astros would simply step over the team to the north, turning the Rangers into an afterthought and winning the first World Series in the state's history. In 2016, though, the Astros went just 4–15 against the Rangers and were held back by their two-year struggle against the AL West leader.

Long-term reinforcements began to arrive in July. They would not save the Astros' season. But Yuli Gurriel was signed and Alex Bregman was promoted to the major leagues in the same month, eventually giving the Astros two more key names that would make major impacts in 2017.

Bregman was only 22, had been drafted No. 2 overall just 13 months earlier, had played just 62 games at Double A and only been a Triple A Fresno Grizzlie for 18 contests. But Springer Day in 2014 had been followed by Correa Day in 2015 for the reconstructed Astros, and Bregman Day—July 25, 2016, against the New York Yankees at Minute Maid Park—completed the final piece of a young Core Four that would be playing in a World Series just 15 months later. Roger Clemens and Andy Pettitte were back at the Astros' ballpark when Bregman debuted, and fans proudly holding up signs arrived early to celebrate another critical addition to the Astros' puzzle.

"We had to be pretty bad for a few years to get to these players," said Hinch, perfectly summing up the Astros' massive rebuild in one sentence.

Astros fans had been begging for Bregman, who had hit .300 with 24 home runs, 35 doubles, 95 RBIs, 108 runs, 20 stolen bases, and an .891 OPS in 146 combined minor league games. As Bregman did everything for the first time with the Astros—pick up a glove, throw to first, eat Springer's candy—a legion of clicking cameras and eyeballs followed his every move.

"It's awesome. It's what you dream about. The team that they have here already is unbelievable," said Bregman, who went 0-for-4 during his debut but came within feet of a grand slam when he lifted a deep fly ball to right field.

The Astros' next asset would take longer to arrive. But just as Bregman's debut set up the increased depth and athleticism that marked a significantly stronger 2017 team, the arrival of Gurriel signaled a head start on off-season free agency and a new line of thinking from the Astros' front office: writing big checks and getting the one guy everyone else wanted to get.

Jim Crane's once painfully cheap ballclub finally stepped up to the financial plate with the Gurriel signing. The largest contract that the Astros had previously handed out during the Luhnow-Crane era was a three-year, $30 million deal for starter/reliever Scott Feldman in December 2013. David Price got $217 million to provide the Red Sox with a 3.99 ERA in 2016. Clayton Kershaw was making $34.5 million to throw a baseball for a living in Los Angeles in 2016. Gurriel's payday didn't completely alter the Astros' overall mid-market tendencies. But a team located in the fourth-largest city in America was finally beginning to act like a big-market pennant contender, all while getting a head start on 2017.

It was a move the Rangers normally made; it was what the Los Angeles Dodgers, Chicago Cubs, and New York Yankees usually did. The Astros had previously pursued international free agents José Abreu and Masahiro Tanaka, coming up short both times. After five years of ticket buyers, at-home fans, and media members pushing the Astros to spend more and back the young talent they already had, the surprise Gurriel signing was a sign of bigger names still to come.

The 2016 Astros needed immediate help, though, and as Bregman struggled with his initial MLB stay (1-for-32 to begin his career) the Cuban-born Gurriel was sent to the minors to adjust to his new baseball life.

With Minute Maid Park just a few hours away, Astros fans called out Gurriel's name and requested selfies at Whataburger Field, which housed the big-league organization's Double A affiliate, the Corpus Christi Hooks. Gurriel was exhausted from cross-country travel and still adjusting to his new environment. Still, Astros minor league coaches immediately praised his smooth but explosive bat. A major league call-up was only a matter of time. "It's inevitable to dream about it. It's been a dream of mine for a long time," Gurriel said, via a translator.

Despite two new names that hinted of future heights, the Astros also went backward in July. They had cut an 11-game deficit to just two-and-a-half by the 22nd. But they finished 13–12 during the month and were six games behind the Rangers on July 31—a day that featured ex-Astro Lucas Harrell pick up the win for Texas. The year prior, Luhnow had traded for three players as the Astros pushed toward the playoffs for the first time in a decade. They had reached the postseason, but neither of the moves had made the major impact that was expected. A year later, the Astros were hesitant to buy heavy as the August 1 trade deadline approached, believing the Rangers were the better team and already moving the big picture toward 2017.

Still, when the AL West leader doubled down and the Astros barely did anything—after entering the spring boasting of World Series goals—the home dugout and clubhouse inside Minute Maid Park were noticeably subdued. Hinch's calm and cool approach became blunt and matter-of-fact. And while Luhnow insisted the Astros were still in full-on win-now mode, the general manager also acknowledged there was no way his club would have done what the Rangers just did.

All-Star catcher Jonathan Lucroy was now a division-race Ranger. So was ex-Astro Carlos Beltran. And while the Cleveland Indians, Toronto Blue Jays, Boston Red Sox, and Chicago Cubs, among others, were big buyers before the non-waiver trade deadline, the Astros sent Feldman to Toronto and did not immediately improve their big-league team. The Astros' uneven balance of the present and future had only continued. The franchise wanted to win it all, right?

"I know it's highly unsatisfying for fans when we don't make big moves at the deadline, especially when other teams do. I get that. I understand that," Luhnow said. "It's highly unsatisfying for you all as the media and for, I'm sure, some of our owners and maybe our players. But the reality is we're doing what we think is the right thing for the organization."

The Astros' Rangers problem—a year away from being erased—also returned to the spotlight. "Texas took three of their top five prospects out of their system to improve....We are not prepared to do that for our organization at this point in time," Luhnow said.

A time would come when the Astros would go all-in (and still retain their youth). But at the 2016 non-waiver deadline, the season-long drive to erase the still-raw memories of a Game 4 ALDS collapse against the Royals ended. The Rangers had bet on themselves. The Astros were sticking with what they already had—which included Bregman and would soon feature Gurriel's major league debut on August 21—and keeping their focus on 2017 and beyond.

"We're not worried about our window shutting," Luhnow said. "We're just getting into our window, so we want to keep it open as long as possible....The lack of moves is a reflection of that mindset."

Still, what the Rangers had done and the Astros had not wasn't ignored by Houston's baseball team.

"That shows that they're wanting to go out and better their team," Rasmus said. "They've already beaten us with what they had. I don't doubt in our team that we can beat them on a given day. But that does show something that they're going out and doing that."

7

OPENING DAY NEXT YEAR

We are proud of the accomplishments and how much the orga-
nization has progressed since 2011. But at the same time, we
also know that success is fleeting and what we really need to
deliver is a championship. We haven't gotten there yet. That's
still our goal—not just one but multiple championships. And
we have to work harder, now that we're in a position where we
see it in front of us...to make sure that we deliver it.

—Jeff Luhnow

CARLOS BELTRAN WAS a Ranger. Lance McCullers Jr. was injured.
A 2016 season that never felt right for the Astros became more and
more uneven during the final two months of the regular season.

McCullers was placed on the disabled list on August 3, two days
after a non-waiver trade deadline that saw the Astros do nothing to
improve their up-and-down big-league team. When McCullers hit
the DL, the Astros were five-and-a-half games behind the first-place
Rangers in the American League West. By mid-August, the deficit
would reach $10^1/_2$.

McCullers had burned through July, striking out 44 in $30^1/_3$
innings while only allowing seven earned runs. But his last start
was August 2, and he did not take the mound again in 2016 for the
Astros. It was another sign a team that began the year with World
Series hopes was already moving its focus toward making a real
run in 2017. "It's not up to me at all," said McCullers, who went
6–5 with a 3.22 ERA but was limited to just 14 total starts in 2016.

"They're taking full control of the process, which is kind of what they should do. I'm really at their mercy."

Beltran just kept on going. He was 39, still making hard contact and still playing for winners. In four months, he would sign with a familiar team that needed his veteran presence and expertise. But for now, the former Astro/Royal/Met/Giant/Cardinal/Yankee was suddenly a Ranger and back in Houston at Minute Maid Park. Beltran's current and past baseball lives were becoming intertwined.

It had been 12 long seasons—five more teams, annual MVP votes, eight All-Star honors—since a 27-year-old who literally could not miss in October 2004 departed last-minute to New York and broke Houston's heart. "He rivals [Albert] Pujols with the most boos," manager A.J. Hinch said.

"I know fans feel like I left because of whatever," said a revived Beltran, who hit .295 with 29 home runs, 93 RBIs, and an .850 OPS in 151 combined games with the Rangers and Yankees in 2016. "People can say anything. But the reality is I was very happy here."

To Astros shortstop Carlos Correa, Beltran was one of the greatest players to come out of Puerto Rico and one of the best switch-hitters in the history of major league baseball. "He inspired a lot of people back home," Correa said. "He inspired me to play the game the right way."

In early August, Beltran paid tribute to the legendary names he initially wore an Astros uniform with: Craig Biggio, Jeff Bagwell, Lance Berkman, Roger Clemens, Roy Oswalt, and Andy Pettitte. Then Beltran explained his side of the late-night decision that still had Astros believers fiercely booing him more than a decade later. "At the end of the year, my mentality was I wanted to stay—I wanted to stay," Beltran said. "But, unfortunately, the ownership didn't want to give me the no-trade clause. As a player, you want security. You want to make a commitment to the city and at the same time make sure that you play there for X amount of years, without worrying about trades and things like that."

A blistering .435 average, eight homers, 14 RBIs, 1.557 OPS, and six stolen bases during 12 postseason games in 2004 were, at that point, Beltran's lasting tribute to the Astros. "It's been 12 years, brother," said Beltran, referring to the boos that still surrounded his name. "Honestly, there's a lot of things that I don't even remember, other than the great playoff that I had. Regular-season stuff that I did over there, I don't remember....But, hey, it is what it is. It's baseball. Baseball should be fun." It was not even a thought then. But baseball would soon be a blast again between Beltran and the Astros, and all he would have to do is change clubhouses—again.

But the 2016 Astros after the deadline? Worn down, beat up, and falling again. They dropped six of seven games from August 2 to 8—including another series to the Rangers—then lost five consecutive contests during the middle of the month. Second place in the AL West was also no longer guaranteed. The Seattle Mariners were locking into that spot, which left third for a fading team that was supposed to compete for a world title.

The Astros were still playing with heart and had not come close to giving in. But they were also aching and barely holding everything together. "We're a beat-up team," said Hinch, after a 5–3 loss to the Rangers in 11 innings on August 7 cracked the Astros a little more.

When the day began, the Astros' No. 5–9 hitters were batting .228, .174, .127, .228, and .207. When it was over, the Astros had scored just 17 runs in their last nine games. Meanwhile, the team on the other side of the field lacked holes and just kept attacking. "They put the ball in play," Hinch said. "They're not a high-strike-out team. They're not a high-walk team, either. So they're going to do their damage with the bats....They've got a good offense."

Jeff Banister's Rangers had been five-and-a-half games out of first place at the same time in 2015, then kept fighting to take the division. Hinch's Astros were just two games off that mark in 2016. But the distance between the clubs had only grown wider at the recent trade deadline, and it was the most the Astros had felt out of the race since their April stumble.

The back-and-forth of the Astros' rebuild—talent, potential, opening a title window…roster holes, question marks, years devoted to losing—returned again as the 2016 campaign wound down. Due to injuries and a lack of production from key veterans, Hinch was forced to turn to young or unproven names during the season's final months. Alex Bregman, A.J. Reed, Tyler White, Joe Musgrove, James Hoyt, Chris Devenski, and Yuli Gurriel all saw key time. Some shined and began building a path toward 2017. Others just struggled. But the Astros were ultimately relying on multiple major league players with little to no October experience.

More than a quarter of the Astros' 25-man roster was under first-year MLB status. Seven rookies (Michael Feliz, Bregman, Reed, White, Musgrove, Hoyt, and Devenski) were proving their major league worth in the public eye, while a wild-card berth and the division title were still up for grabs. Several of the Astros' young arms stepped up and aided the team in 2016. But many of the bats had disappointed, again highlighting a lineup in need of more contact hitters and overall consistency from 1–9.

"Part of our recent offensive struggles is not just due to the rookies," Luhnow said. "It's also due to the fact that our veterans hadn't been playing the way they had been playing the last couple months. Typically, the easiest way to break in a rookie is lower in the lineup, with veterans in the middle of the lineup who are carrying most of the load."

Most first-year players struggle when they arrive in the majors. Correa was the exception. Everyone from Mike Trout and Craig Biggio to Ryne Sandberg and Willie Mays had needed time to shine. "We were hoping that our run of success with our young players would continue," Luhnow said. "I still think our young players are going to be a big part of the rest of this year and the future. But there has been a trend this year where they have come up and they haven't impacted the game right out of the gate."

For Banister, the needs of his Rangers team dictated the right balance of youth with known names. "I know that the youth, or the young guys, they're the guys that drive the energy bus for us," Banister said. "And the veterans are the stabilizers—they're the glue that holds it all together."

He also acknowledged there was no perfect plan in the complex world of modern major league baseball. "I don't believe there's any real magic formula to say this is the right amount or wrong amount," Banister said. "I think when you look up at the end of the year and kind of look over different World Series champions, they all are made differently."

Premier clubs such as the Chicago Cubs, Washington Nationals, Baltimore Orioles, and Boston Red Sox were relying on youth to win in 2016. Almost every club in both pennant races was bolstered by proven vets and higher payrolls, though. Hinch acknowledged the Astros' reliance on youth in a division race was "different." But he stressed the team's young underachievers could break out at any time, and experience did not always equal consistent productivity.

In 2016 disappointing veteran bats and unpredictable young hitters thrust onto the major league stage resulted in an uneven lineup that ranked 24th among 30 teams in batting average (.247) and 14th in OPS (.735) and home runs (198). A year later, some of those same young bats would blossom, while a much-improved lineup would turn the Astros into the best-hitting team in baseball. In August 2016, though, the rough edges of the Astros' rebuild were still evident.

"It's harder on the players because they're trying to speed up their learning curve that is necessary at the big-league level, in order to feel better," Hinch said. "The steep learning curve that can be the jump from Triple A to the big leagues, a lot of us are responsible for. Coaches, me as the manager, players. It's a continual grind to get guys to feel comfortable at this level, first, and then productive next."

Even with all the young names, they had one more run in them. The streaky, sometimes frustrating, sometimes thrilling 2016 Astros pulled within one game of the American League's final wild-card spot as September approached.

"I feel really confident with our club. Our boys, they're finally turning the corner right now," said closer Ken Giles, who locked down the ninth during a 4–3 home win against Oakland, which gave the Astros a series sweep of the Athletics, slimmed Giles' ERA to a then season-low 3.54, and helped his team improve to 71–62.

Thirteen upcoming contests against MLB's elite teams (the Rangers, Indians, Cubs, and Rangers again) awaited. A strong finish to August had given the Astros new life, and if they could survive their September 2–14 public trial, all the lingering issues in 2016 might end up being forgotten. "It means we're good," Hinch said. "We can be better, and we're going to keep trying to be better. We're not a perfect team. But we've got a group that is pretty resilient....There's a fight in this group that's fun to watch and fun to be around."

They had been resilient. But, overall, they just did not have enough. The Astros dropped eight of their initial 12 games in September and were 75–70 after another loss to the Rangers. They went 12–15 in a month that, like April, defined a disappointing season.

The Astros hosted the eventual World Series–winning Cubs from September 9 to 11 at Minute Maid Park. In Chicago, Houston was presented with a stronger, more win-now version of itself. The Cubs had young talent that would last for years. Like the Astros, they had built around youthful names but were also aggressively pursuing the franchise's first championship in 108 years. The best team in baseball in 2016 had lost 101 games just four years ago during a top-to-bottom rebuild. Now, they were set to make the playoffs for the second consecutive year and were being lauded as one of baseball's ideal contemporary franchises.

Theo Epstein, Jed Hoyer, Joe Maddon, and the Ricketts family showed the Astros a future version of themselves a year in advance of Houston's first world title. The Cubs developed their own talent, spent big-city money, and made major trades that improved the big-league team. Second (and third) place were for losers.

"I see them with more wins," Hinch joked. "That makes me jealous." Then he examined the similarities and differences between two clubs that had much more in common than not. "As we continue to see some of the younger players come up and make an impact, you can see why we were so infatuated with building the farm system up and so excited for the future—the future is now," Hinch said. "The Cubs did the same thing. They've added to it a little bit through free agency and a few trades and have built their team a touch differently than we have."

The Cubs also possessed a modernized Wrigley Field, an iconic national brand, and the fifth highest payroll in baseball ($182 million).

"They have a much higher revenue," Luhnow said. "That's a plus and a minus. It leads to high expectations, and they have to deliver—and they have. This group's done an unbelievable job. I can't think of anything they've done really wrong....Clearly, they're going to be a force to be reckoned with for a long time."

The Astros were focused on being an annual contender first, then going for the whole thing. When they were ready for the next step, they swore they would make the necessary moves and spend their "powder." The Cubs were simply a year ahead in their reconstruction. "Both organizations have the same approach of trying to build from within and then complement that with players through trades and free agency," Luhnow said. "The other important element to both of our [plans] has been communicating with the fans and setting expectations."

For all the comparisons—Astros-Rangers, Astros-Cubs—and constant swings throughout 2016, the season finally came down to one fact: the as-is Astros were just not good enough. By late September, Luis Valbuena, Dallas Keuchel, McCullers, and Bregman were out of sight. The Rangers had proved for the second consecutive season that they were the best baseball team in Texas—division winners who were unafraid to spend major cash and make big moves like an October contender. Hinch's beat-up club was barely hanging on at the end of a chaotic six-month marathon. The Astros' lineup struck out too much, did not score enough, failed to reach base consistently, and often struggled just to make contact. The rotation and bullpen were both unreliable, lacking the precision and power of 2015.

A year before, the Astros had also been 81–74 after 155 games. But there was no lasting magic in 2016 and even the final wild-card spot was about to be out of sight. For the second straight year, Hinch had done more with less. And in 2016 José Altuve and Correa had been forced to carry too much weight for too long.

It all ended with an 84–78 mark and third place in the AL West. They were just two wins off their 2015 total, but the Astros knew that 2016 was an internal wake-up call. They were not winning a World Series unless the entire team improved and the organization acted like it was all-in, instead of just saying it.

In 2016, the show ended before Game 160 began, and the Astros' final series barely meant anything. A season after Luhnow and Hinch had silently consoled each other following an AL Division Series defeat to the eventual world champion Kansas City Royals, it was just the skipper and the general manager sitting behind a plain table at Minute Maid Park, explaining how their team was going to take the big step that fans had been waiting for. "I'm not

handling it very well at all, to be honest," Hinch said. "I hate losing....But I'm proud of the fact that 84 wins isn't good enough.
And I'm proud of the fact that the standards have risen in the two
years since I've been here."

After coming within six outs of the AL Championship Series in
2015, the Astros now had to create a path to something much bigger, and they had a playoff-free off-season for all of the necessary
work. "We are as motivated as we ever have been....I can't wait 'til
Opening Day next year," said Luhnow, who was 346–464 while
running the Astros.

Owner Jim Crane's franchise had finished sixth (NL Central),
fifth (AL West), fourth, second, and third in its division since Luhnow's reconstruction began. The Astros had clearly proved they
could be a good—and at times very dangerous—team the last two
years. But they were also several critical pieces away from entering
2017 as a true World Series contender. As they prepared to enter a
new spring training home in West Palm Beach, Florida, baseball's
surprise team in 2015 was surrounded by critical question marks.
"It's going to be tough. We're going to have a tough division," Luhnow said. "I think we're well-positioned for next year. There are
very few organizations of the 30 that have quite as exciting a young
core to build around, and really, that's our job this off-season."

The Astros had a shot in every game just by writing George
Springer, Altuve, Correa, Bregman, and more into the daily lineup.
Their window was clearly open, and their future was not limited
by expiring veteran contracts or loaded down with outrageously
expensive multiyear deals. But, outside of the Gurriel signing, they
also had not displayed the mindset of a real buyer. As the 2016
season ended for the Astros, there was still a clear divide that separated them from the Rangers, Cubs, Red Sox, Dodgers, and more.

Luhnow offered encouraging words, though, in early October
and hinted at the changes to come after his team fell short of the
playoffs. "Between the dollars that are coming off from [our] free

agents and the increase in payroll that Jim is willing to provide... we're going to have the resources to go out and sign some players," he said.

After the Cubs and Indians went seven games in one of the best World Series in the sport's history, the Astros went to work on their self-improvement. They won the off-season, which eventually helped bring Justin Verlander to Houston and deliver the first World Series title in franchise history.

Crane, Luhnow, Hinch, and the already-under-construction 2017 Astros quick-pitched the rest of MLB, adding two much-needed veterans, Brian McCann and Josh Reddick, in the same week. The sight of multiple free-agent additions by the local nine in mid-November was almost six years in the making. From 324 total defeats in 2011–2013 to baseball's best surprise in 2015. From a step backward in 2016 and another Rangers division crown to the most aggressive franchise in the big leagues before the winter meetings had even fired up.

The rebuild was now just part of the past. The 2017 season was going to set up all the years that followed. "This year we're going to put ourselves in the position where we have a few more safety nets and we surround our young core with some proven veteran players that are able to contribute," Luhnow said. "We think that gives us our best possible chance of success this year, without giving up a ton of our future potential in the three- to seven-year timetable."

McCann and Reddick had big, baseball-devoted markets New York, Boston, and Los Angeles between them and 11 total postseason runs to their names. They had been there and done it. It took $52 million for four years to turn Reddick from a late-season playoff Dodger into an Astro. It required a couple of pitching prospects to bring McCann, a former Brave and Yankee, south again. It was new ground for Houston's baseball club—and how true contenders operated every year. Crane had green-lighted a payroll increase, and the Astros quickly went to work to fill in their holes.

"Our ownership group has been incredibly supportive," Luhnow said. "[They] let the baseball operations people do what they do to improve the team and provide us with the resources that we need to get better."

Hinch's lineup was instantly deeper, and the clubhouse had added respected veteran names. If the Astros slid in 2017, someone would pick them up. Factor in internal improvement from young stars and a bounce-back year from 2015 AL Cy Young Award winner Dallas Keuchel, and the Astros were already threatening the Rangers before 2017 had even begun. Then there was the quiet signing of veteran right-hander Charlie Morton for $14 million over two years. If the Astros could keep Morton healthy, their rotation could match their lineup in the new year.

"We need to do the best job possible to give our players and our fans a chance to win a championship, and that's what we've been doing," Luhnow said. "We've been pursuing that aggressively, and I think our fans are going to see the results of that starting this year on the field."

Fans also would not be booing Beltran anymore. The Astros officially became baseball's hottest team in December, when they brought the former Astro back to Houston on a one-year, $16 million deal. A top-heavy 2016 lineup was now completely loaded for 2017, and the Astros had added the clubhouse veterans they were clearly missing. Beltran was rejoining a team that appeared to be just a few pieces away when the off-season began. Now Hinch could move names and spots around all winter, perfecting a lineup that would give opposing arms trouble for all 162 games.

After five years of building toward this point, the 2017 Astros could not arrive soon enough.

2017 Houston Astros

Record: 101–61

Manager: A.J. Hinch **General Manager:** Jeff Luhnow **Owner:** Jim Crane
Playoffs : Astros 3-1 over Boston Red Sox in American League Divisions Series; Astros 4-3 over New York Yankees in AL Championship Series; Astros 4-3 over Los Angeles Dodgers in World Series
Awards: José Altuve, AL MVP; George Springer, World Series MVP

World Series Roster *(All-Stars in **bold**)*

Player	Position	2017 Team Stats	Acquired
Yuli Gurriel	1B	.299 BA, 18 HR, 75 RBIs	Free agent 2016
José Altuve	2B	.346 BA, 24 HR, 81 RBIs	Free agent 2006
Carlos Correa	SS	.315 BA, 24 HR, 84 RBIs	Draft 2012 (No. 1)
Alex Bregman	3B	.284 BA, 19 HR, 71 RBIs	Draft 2015 (No. 2)
Brian McCann	C	.241 BA, 18 HR, 62 RBIs	Trade 2016
Evan Gattis	C/DH	.263 BA, 12 HR, 55 RBIs	Trade 2015
Josh Reddick	RF	.314 BA, 13 HR, 82 RBIs	Free agent 2016
George Springer	CF	.283 BA, 34 HR, 85 RBIs	Draft 2011 (No. 11)
Marwin González	OF/INF	.303 BA, 23 HR, 90 RBIs	Trade 2011
Carlos Beltran	DH	.231 BA, 14 HR, 51 RBIs	Free agent 2016
Derek Fisher	OF	.212 BA, 5 HR, 17 RBIs	Draft 2014 (No. 37)
Cameron Maybin	OF	.186 BA, 4 HR, 13 RBIs	Waivers 2017
Juan Centeno	C	.231 BA, 2 HR, 4 RBIs	Free agent 2016
Justin Verlander	P	5–0, 1.06 ERA, 43 K	Trade 2017
Dallas Keuchel	P	14–5, 2.90 ERA, 125 K	Draft 2009
Charlie Morton	P	14–7, 3.62 ERA, 163 K	Free agent 2016
Lance McCullers Jr.	P	7–4, 4.25 ERA, 132 K	Draft 2012 (No. 41)
Brad Peacock	P	13–2, 3.00 ERA, 161 K	Trade 2013
Collin McHugh	P	5–2, 3.55 ERA, 62 K	Waivers 2013
Ken Giles	P	1–3, 2.30 ERA, 34 S	Trade 2015
Chris Devenski	P	8–5, 2.68 ERA, 62 G	Trade 2012
Will Harris	P	3–2, 2.98 ERA, 46 G	Waivers 2014
Luke Gregerson	P	2–3, 4.57 ERA, 65 G	Free agent 2014
Joe Musgrove	P	7–8, 4.77 ERA, 38 G	Trade 2012
Francisco Liriano	P	0–2, 4.40 ERA, 20 G	Trade 2017

Key Contributors
Position players: Jake Marisnick, Nori Aoki, J.D. Davis, Tyler White. **Pitchers:** Mike Fiers, Tony Sipp, Michael Feliz, James Hoyt, Francis Martes, Reymin Guduan, Tyler Clippard, Dayan Diaz.

8

WHEN THE STAR GOES UP

All I can be is my best self. And where the leadership feels that fits in to the organization is up to them. Jim [Crane] and Jeff [Luhnow] have been great to me. But I know this sport— sports—is about winning. I know that the expectations, as they raise, the microscope starts to come to me. And to be honest with you, I prefer it to be on me than I do the players. My job is to lead this team.

—A.J. Hinch

UNDER CONSTRUCTION.

They always were, really. Even as Jeff Luhnow entered his sixth season as the Astros' architect. Even with the deepest, strongest, and most talented roster that A.J. Hinch had ever possessed—and that was before Justin Verlander agreed to wrap himself in orange and blue at the last possible minute.

The 2017 Astros were on major league baseball's World Series radar before they even arrived in West Palm Beach, Florida. When they did, they were surrounded by construction crews, pickup trucks, cement mixers, and mounds of dirt.

A massive, unprecedented rebuild had reached a new pivotal stage.

After 32 years of holding spring training in Kissimmee, Florida, Jim Crane had fulfilled another early promise by relocating his baseball team to Florida's southeast coast. Mickey Mouse, Disney World, and all those days stuck in pointless traffic belonged to the Astros' past life at Osceola County Stadium. José Altuve, George

Springer, Carlos Correa, and Alex Bregman now shared a state-of-the-art complex with Bryce Harper's Washington Nationals. Of course, the sparkling stadium with the only-in-Florida name—The Ballpark of the Palm Beaches—was still being finished as the 2017 Astros were cracking wood and heating up their arms for the first time.

There were singing birds, swaying palm trees, and a constant ocean breeze. It was postcard-perfect, mid-February sunshine and a huge Astros H, backed by an orange star, out front that lit up every night.

The birds were also there for a reason: the team's new home away from home was built on a garbage dump. And along with a practice field that replicated the dimensions of Minute Maid Park and all the 70-inch, plastic-covered HDTVs, there were large collections of new things still contained in taped-up boxes, electrical cords still waiting to be connected, and a sign out front that read "Construction Area—KEEP OUT."

"There's a lot of pride when the star goes up at the front," said Marcel Braithwaite, Astros senior vice president of business operations. "When that was lit up at night and it reflected back on the lake, we took a couple pictures, and we were like, 'Okay. It's real. This is home.'"

The Astros' projected $123 million Opening Day payroll was finally real money for a franchise that had intentionally hit rock bottom—on the field and with its MLB cash flow—just four years ago. The spring of 2017 began with Dallas Keuchel peeking through blinds and jokingly flexing his muscles for reporters—the 2015 American League Cy Young Award winner was coming off a disappointing 2016, when he went just 9–12 with a 4.55 ERA and only threw 168 innings—while Hinch was dreaming up where he wanted everything on a previously untouched dry-erase board.

The reconstructed Astros had almost everything they needed to rise to the top of baseball in 2017. But they were still missing a few key pieces and had cracked from their own internal pressure a year ago. "What gets me out of bed every morning is not fear of the pressure that comes in professional sports," Hinch said. "It's a burning desire to bring a championship to these players, to our fans, to this organization."

Bregman arrived before everyone, as the construction chaos was still pounding away. "Baseball rat," Hinch called him. It was baseball, so that was a term of affection and public praise for a 22-year-old who had gone 1-for-32 after a much-hyped July 2016 call-up, then battled back to finish his rookie season hitting .264 with eight home runs, 13 doubles, 34 RBIs, and a .791 OPS in 49 games. "Expectations are high," Luhnow said. "This is a guy who was in college two years ago, and he's penciled into our everyday lineup right now. It's a hard transition to make. But if anybody can make it, I think Alex can."

Veteran reliever Luke Gregerson opened up piled-up boxes while cracking jokes. Closer Ken Giles proudly discussed the off-season muscle weight he had intentionally added. Ex-Yankee Brian McCann warmly hugged just-married Evan Gattis, with the two short-haired and thickly-bearded catchers suddenly looking like twins inside the Astros' new spring training clubhouse.

Bregman walked through a room that was still waking up, coffee cup in hand. It was just another day on the job in mid-February, during a Hollywood-like season that would run through November 1 and end up as the greatest year in franchise history.

"What's up?" the baseball rat said.

While the top shelf of every other new locker was still empty and clean, Bregman's was already loaded with wood. The weekend before pitchers and catchers reported, the No. 2 overall pick of the 2015 amateur draft was already showing up daily at the ballpark, getting a head start on 2017. "I'm just obsessed with [baseball]," Bregman said. "It's all I want to do every day. I love it. I love my job. I feel very fortunate every single day to be able to do that, so I'm not going to take a day off."

In early October, Bregman would lean on the top railing inside the visitor's dugout at Fenway Park, shouting in the cold rain as the Astros roared back in Game 4 of the American League Division Series to suddenly end Boston's season. A few weeks before spring training began, Springer was teasing his young teammate about an odd pregame ritual: Bregman arriving for 7:10 PM home starts at noon, walking around with batting gloves already on and then being in full uniform before every other teammate.

"I don't know why you do that, but you do," Springer joked.

Hinch demanded full dedication and fewer mental mistakes from everyone in 2017. This season's Astros would be sharper. "We will always play hard under my watch," he said. "It's a simple rule. It's expected....That's a given at this level for this team. The close games that we lost last year, it was not an issue with effort, it was not an issue with preparation, it was not an issue with the players being focused....But the small moments within the game, we have to be better. And last year, early, we played well enough to lose by a little. And those games hurt us in the end."

The third-year manager also saw what stood out the clearest inside a modern complex in need of some dirt.

Carlos Beltran. Josh Reddick. McCann.

Verlander was still more than six months away from forever changing the Astros' world. But a team that had been battered by the in-state rival Texas Rangers the last two seasons now had three proven veterans who knew there was more to a major league season than just winning the AL West.

Hinch's initial two teams had lacked veteran leadership, playoff experience, and contact bats. Luhnow had responded by providing the manager with the makings of the best lineup in baseball. Within the clubhouse walls, Beltran, McCann, and Reddick brought the intangibles that are invaluable, even in the wildly overpriced world of modern major league baseball.

"We've come a long way since 2012," Luhnow said. "It took us 10 years to get back to the playoffs, and we did it with some pretty exciting young players....We've got to build around that young core."

Bregman and Correa were only 22, Altuve was 26, and Springer was 27. A *Houston Chronicle* picture of the foursome united and standing together in West Palm Beach—Bregman smiling with his arm around a confident Altuve, Correa and Springer as bookends in peak athletic shape—captured the franchise-altering potential of the Astros' young Core Four.

Beltran, 39, fit in with the kids the moment he walked through the front door, which tells you everything about just how tight the Astros' chemistry had become under Hinch—and what the club was missing during the initial two years after the 100-loss seasons. "The life lessons that he's learned along the way are irreplaceable. He's willing to give that back to any of our players," said Hinch, who played with Beltran on the 2001–2002 Kansas City Royals. "We want him to be a good player. A lot is going to be said about the impact that he has behind the scenes. I don't want to shorten the impact that we need him to have on the field. And he's still putting up really good numbers—Father Time is not affecting him like it does most of us."

Beltran pulled back a crisp orange-and-blue cap, showing off a mostly shaved head. "Well, I got no hair," he said, smiling. "What else? We can go on and on."

McCann shook the hand of a fellow former Yankee, then pulled in for a friendly embrace. Altuve, Springer, and Bregman surrounded the ex-Ranger in the batting cage, never letting Beltran out of their sight. When Beltran finished his first round in the cage, he intentionally walked behind Springer and patted the Astros' center fielder on the back. When the Astros moved to the back fields,

Beltran sat between Marwin González and Altuve on the grass, telling an inside story that bridged generations and decades.

The mind of infield instructor Adam Everett jumped back to the glory of 2004, when Beltran was an Astro who could do no wrong and hit almost everything fired his way, scorching the baseball earth for two weeks during one of the greatest playoff runs the game has seen. After all those years of being mercilessly booed at Minute Maid Park for leaving the Astros for the New York Mets in January 2005, the team needed the aging designated hitter more than ever.

"He comes up and gives me a hug, which is great. But the way he embraced the younger players—this guy's not faking it," said Everett, who spent 2001–2007 playing for the Astros and watched Beltran hit .435 with eight home runs, 14 RBIs, six stolen bases, and a 1.557 OPS in the 2004 postseason.

McCann was just as essential. Steady, calm, and tested. Nine MLB years in Atlanta and three with the Yankees had turned the 33-year-old into a gritty veteran who had seen it all and would have easily fit on any team in baseball's past eras.

"I love this guy," Beltran said. "He's the best—the best."

Reddick came from a different world, but also instantly blended in. The 912 area code for Savannah, Georgia, was thickly tattooed on his left arm in black ink. Spider-Man T-shirts and webbed superhero costumes hung inside the locker of a 30-year-old man. But Reddick also willingly crashed into outfield walls, ran out grounders, and gunned out would-be advancers from right field. He played the game hard. And after playing in only 115 games combined for Oakland and the Dodgers in 2016, the veteran booed by Los Angeles' fans quickly found a new home with the Astros.

"Being in this lineup is just something special to be a part of," Reddick said. "You look at the guys who are starting things off, and I'm sitting here wondering where I'm going to hit. I'm excited no matter where it is. I could be hitting sixth and it'd be like hitting third."

The bats would spend the next nine months carrying the Astros to the World Series.

"When we're at our best, we have a little bit of everything," Hinch said. "Our contact skills are going to be better. Our situational hitting is going to be better. And we've got a chance to do damage all the way through the lineup....We're going to be able to come at you from nine-strong, and then have guys on the bench who could arguably play every day."

But what about the arms?

When the club crashed in the 2015 playoffs, it was because the bullpen fell apart. In 2016 starters Lance McCullers Jr. and Keuchel were limited by injuries, and their team—which went 18–8 in June and spent time as the hottest squad in baseball—faded in September. A year after combining for just 40 starts, the Astros entered a new season leaning on Keuchel and McCullers more than ever. And for all the improvements made to a bullpen that posted the highest ERA in the game in 2013 and 2014, everyone from Chris Devenski and Joe Musgrove to Giles took the mound in West Palm Beach with something to prove.

"You look at the Cubs [in 2016]," Keuchel said. "They had a great staff the whole year in the regular season. That's how you're going to win 100-plus games. You're going to score a lot of runs with the Rangers. But if they would have had a couple more starters...they would have had 100 wins."

McCullers had been one of the best pitchers in baseball in July 2016, posting a 2.08 ERA while striking out 44 in 30⅓ innings, as the Astros attempted to erase a backward 7–17 start that sabotaged a season loaded with increased expectations. He only threw one more game the rest of the year, though, and rivaled Keuchel as the team's biggest question mark on the mound entering 2017. "There were different times last year where the different parts of the team showed up," McCullers said. "It's the most important thing…to kind of be clicking all at the same time, especially toward the end when you're trying to make that run."

Charlie Morton, a nine-year veteran quietly signed during the off-season, had only thrown four games for a 91-loss Philadelphia team the year prior. Brad Peacock, oft-injured and regularly bouncing between the majors and minors ever since the rebuilding Astros traded for him in February 2013, had been limited to 11 total games in 2015–2016.

But as the lockers filled up and eager fans got their first glimpse of the 2017 Astros in the Florida sun, Keuchel and McCullers were adamant that this year's team had enough on the mound to return to the postseason.

"The five guys we will have will be enough to win the West and to make a playoff run. I firmly believe that," the 2015 American League Cy Young Award winner said.

That belief took a hit before Game 1 of 162 even arrived.

Right-hander Collin McHugh had gone 19–7 with a 3.89 ERA in 2015 during the Astros' first playoff run in a decade, becoming a key early name on an ever-growing list of castoffs that Luhnow's staff pulled from the waiver wire. But McHugh did not make his first start of 2017 until July 22, after being shut down with an elbow injury and opening a hole in the middle of the Astros' rotation.

The club was attached to multiple starters via potential trades throughout the off-season, with rumors dating back to the build-up toward the 2016 non-waiver deadline. Nothing real had materialized. When the Astros first took the field for a season that would last until November 1 at Dodger Stadium, their initial rotation was a shell of its World Series self: Keuchel, McCullers, Morton, Joe Musgrove, and Mike Fiers.

"Starting pitching, in general, always feels the responsibility to set the tone," Hinch said. "You never see a winning team not have a really good starting staff. They don't have to be the biggest names; they don't have to be the brightest stars. They have to be the most effective five- to nine-inning pitchers that they can be."

By Game 7 of the World Series, Morton would be called on for four innings of franchise-changing relief, Musgrove and McHugh would be in the pen, while Fiers had not made the cut for the 25-man Fall Classic roster. In West Palm Beach, the team was banking on its depth, yet privately wondering what would happen if too many fill-in names fell through.

But the overriding feelings—in the cages and back fields of a new complex still being unwrapped—were confidence and swagger. And this time, it was for real.

"Getting off to that start in 2015 was huge, because the mindset changed," Hinch said. "And you look back at that now, and we've only played a couple games of irrelevant baseball, which is the last weekend of the season last year. I'm very proud of that. To where we enter the building for year three [and] the players, the coaching staff, the support staff, the front office—the mindset has changed. And the standards have changed, and the expectations obviously come with that."

The heartbeat of the young, fun, and highly addicting Astros from 2015 could still be heard. The majority of the team's holes had also been filled in, and Hinch's club was seeing and feeling the same things the rest of baseball was. They had also spent two seasons building a new world with their manager.

"I love connecting with people. I love connecting with players," Hinch said. "And I just believe to be the most impactful in a relationship, you have to have that relationship....If you build the relationship right, you can do anything you want as a mentor, as a coach, as someone who's trustworthy and that has their best interests at heart."

The Cleveland Indians would be strong again. The world champion Chicago Cubs were not going away. The Los Angeles Dodgers had been building and buying their way toward a World Series for years. The Rangers had owned the AL West two consecutive seasons and were a safe pick for a third straight division crown. But if everything finally came together for Houston's baseball team in 2017 and a franchise once devoted to bottoming out actually acted like a major-market club? Hinch's Astros could turn the playoff promise of 2015 into an international stage that felt impossible just a few years ago.

"We'll have a lot of confidence going in, but we'll also be humble enough to realize you have to go prove it and you have to go earn the distinction," he said. "The last two seasons, the Texas Rangers have won the division, pretty much in our face. Until we beat them and have more wins than them, we can't really brag about anything....But I absolutely like this team."

Hinch's front-office counterpart was equally upbeat by the time West Palm Beach was in the rearview and the Astros were hosting the defending-champion Cubs for a two-game exhibition series in late March at Minute Maid Park.

"This is the most optimistic I've been heading into a season," Luhnow said. "There's very few pieces that I really can think of that I'd like to add right now. And that's a good spot to be for a GM."

On April 3, Houston got its first full look at a team that would remain in its hearts through November, then end up linking 1962 with 1980, 1986, 2005, 2015, and so much more.

A red, white, and, blue Opening Day symbol was painted behind home plate. Tal's Hill had been ripped away and replaced by a wall of plastic ivy, a standing-room-only deck, and a huge orange-and-white H that resembled the Astros' oversized spring-training sign.

The stadium in downtown Houston murmured and buzzed, then exhaled in a unified shout of joy. Keuchel threw seven smooth innings of two-hit, four-strikeout ball for a 1–0 start to 2017. Springer led it all off with a 378-foot homer to left-center field off Seattle's Felix Hernandez. And as the top four batters in the Astros' lineup (Springer, Bregman, Altuve, Correa) all recorded their initial hits of a new season, Keuchel, Gregerson, and Giles blanked the Mariners 3–0 in a sharp shutout before a sold-out crowd of 41,678.

"I always try to get in and out," Keuchel said. "That's my motto. Everybody pays to see the offense, anyways. Nobody really wants to see pitching."

In a scene repeated over and over again throughout October, the stadium stood as one in the seventh after Keuchel gloved his second bunt of the night, then threw sharply off his back foot to end the frame.

The old Keuchel was back.

The best team in Astros history could not have started its world championship season any better.

A spring-training line from Hinch would last all season.

"I will always have the loudest vote in the clubhouse," he said. "But I will also have the calmest heartbeat."

9

PEOPLE ARE JUST WOOING

That's me. What you see is out there....What you see now is what you're going to get. This is a childhood dream still for a lot of us, and I'm going to enjoy it.
— Astros outfielder Josh Reddick

THEY STARTED WINNING and never stopped. But first, they had to remember how to hit.

It's funny now, looking back. The brief moment of concern. That time in early April when 2017 felt like 2016 all over again, and A.J. Hinch was already being questioned about the state of his lineup and dormant bats. How silly.

When the dream season was complete, the Astros would finish with the second-most wins in franchise history, then add 11 more in the playoffs for the first World Series trophy in the city's history. But on April 10, Hinch's club was just 4–4 and again stumbling out of the gate.

Pressure. Expectations. Trying to do too much as one person, instead of playing within the system and sacrificing for the team. That was the early problem in 2016, and the Astros ultimately never recovered. A year later, young stars who swore that 2017 would be different sounded like playoff-proven veterans just a few games into the long 162. "Nothing to worry about....We're going to get back on track and be able to produce," said Carlos Correa, after the Astros dropped their first homestand finale to Seattle and only averaged three runs in four games.

Hinch would echo those words more than six months later, calmly dimming down mounting concern after George Springer went 0-for-4 with four Ks in a Game 1 defeat to the Los Angeles Dodgers in the World Series. "I know George has struggled," Hinch said. "If he hits the first pitch tomorrow into the gap or hits a single or hits the ball out of the ballpark, you'd be amazed how good he feels."

The Astros began 2017 with a 3–1 record, immediately taking over first place in a division that it owned from April through October. But after an off-season drooling over the team's best lineup on paper since the peak of the Jeff Bagwell and Craig Biggio days, José Altuve, Carlos Beltran, Alex Bregman, and Yuli Gurriel started a new season a combined 9-for-58, and it took a 13th-inning homer from Springer for the Astros to survive their third game and take their first series of the year.

"We're going to hit, we're going to score some runs. It's only game four," Springer said. "So once we get back the hang of playing again in this environment, at this speed, we'll be fine."

Talk radio and social media were not as patient. But the real story ended up being the sounds that preceded Springer's walkoff, which was lifted 353 feet to left-center field inside an emptied-out stadium during a game that lasted 4 hours and 25 minutes, and saw the Astros fall behind 3–2 in the top of the 13th, then come within one out in the bottom of the frame from falling to the Mariners.

Just three contests into their 162-game campaign, the Astros had established a storyline that would repeat itself all year—resilience, perseverance, shared belief—and already had a calling card. As Wednesday evening moved toward Thursday morning, the TV broadcast picked up a peculiar late-inning sound from the diminished crowd. Whistling? Booing? Boredom?

Wooing.

Popularized by pro wrestler Ric Flair, the ringing "Wooooooo!" was organically attached to Josh Reddick and the 2017 Astros,

From 2011 to 2013 Houston endured three 100-plus-loss seasons, finishing in last place each time. But there were bright spots during that period—notably the major league debut of José Altuve (top) in 2011, and the drafting of Carlos Correa (right) with the No. 1 overall pick in 2012.

In 2015 Astros GM Jeff Luhnow (left) hired A.J. Hinch as the team's new manager. Since then, Houston has had three straight winning seasons, two playoff appearances, one AL West division title, an American League pennant, and its first ever World Series title.

By 2015 Altuve was already a two-time All-Star and batting champion. With an influx of young talent, Altuve led the Astros to their first playoff appearance since 2005 and added a Gold Glove to his trophy case.

After a strong 2014 season, in 2015 Dallas Keuchel proved himself to be one of the top starting pitchers in baseball, going 20–8 with a 2.48 ERA and 1.017 WHIP. He won the 2015 AL Cy Young Award and shut down the New York Yankees in the wild-card playoff, earning the win with six shutout innings.

Correa and Altuve high-five after the Astros take Game 1 of the 2015 ALDS 5–2 from the home-team Kansas City Royals.

	1	2	3	4	5	6	7	8	9		R
KC	0	2	0	0	0	0	0	4			6
OU	0	1	1	0	1	0	3				6

Up 2–1 in the series and 6–2 going into the eighth inning of Game 4 of the 2015 ALDS, the Astros allowed the Royals to score five runs and take a 7–6 lead in Minute Maid Park. In the ninth, Kansas City first baseman Eric Hosmer belted a two-run home run to make it 9–6. The Royals won the game and clinched the series back home in Game 5, ending the Astros' season.

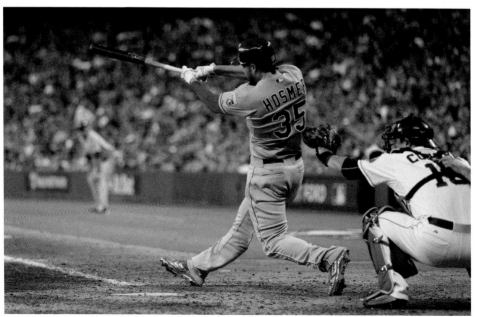

Minutes before the 2017 trade deadline on August 31, GM Jeff Luhnow pulled the trigger on the trade that would put the Astros over the top, acquiring right-handed starting pitcher Justin Verlander from the Detroit Tigers. Verlander went 5–0 in September with a 1.06 ERA.

Astros third baseman Alex Bregman slaps hands with fans at Minute Maid Park after Houston clinched the AL West on September 17, 2017, by beating the Seattle Mariners 7–1.

Astros center fielder George Springer (4) and Altuve (27) celebrate after scoring on Correa's double in the sixth inning of Game 2 of the 2017 ALDS against the Boston Red Sox.

Josh Reddick singles in the eighth inning of Game 4 to drive in the go-ahead run, making it 4–3 Astros, after being down 3–2 on the road and staring down a 2–2 series tie to start the inning.

Astros closer Ken Giles is pumped up after getting the Red Sox's Dustin Pedroia to ground out to end the game, a 5–4 Astros win, giving Houston a 3–1 series victory.

via a grassroots, impromptu movement that eventually became a marketing slogan plastered across T-shirts and Minute Maid Park's jumbotron. "Going back to that first homestand, it's just crazy that fans would even start doing that randomly," Reddick said. "I turned around, and I was like, 'That's kind of weird.' Because I know Texas is a big wrestling state....But I didn't expect it to be a WWE field event, where people are just wooing around. I went home and talked to my buddy. I said, 'Man, if they're out there like that, imagine if I walked up to it the next day.' Sure enough, here we are months later, dealing with it. But it's been great, because it shows you how much they want to get into it."

After years of waiting, the heartbreak of 2015 and the setback in 2016, it was incredibly easy to get into the new season's Astros. They started 10–5, reached 20–10 and turned a 22–7 May into the strongest start in franchise history.

History. That word kept ringing out throughout 2017. With each passing week, then changing month, the Astros had produced a new set of numbers that topped every previous year since it all began in 1962.

In 2015 the Astros were 10 games above .500 in mid-May. But only 21,653 fans—the rest still recovering from all the 100-loss seasons—showed up to watch baseball's biggest early-season surprise. Hinch's first team then spent the rest of the year convincing nonbelievers the reborn Astros were for real.

Two years later, the club led the AL West by eight games in mid-May and was widely accepted as a true playoff contender. A quarter of the way into 162, the Astros ranked third in MLB in batting average (.271) and hits (390), fifth in OPS (.784), and sixth in runs (214). Dallas Keuchel and Lance McCullers Jr. answered spring concerns by guiding a staff that led baseball in batting average against (.228) and was second in ERA (3.45).

"It's still pretty early in the context of the season," said the intentionally cautious Hinch. "I do love the way that we've gone about our business and continued to methodically win some series, and win in different ways and just play good baseball."

After their light-hitting 4–4 beginning, the team rolled off eight wins in nine games and only built off the veteran foundation established during spring training in West Palm Beach. "We have leadership this year and we have great team chemistry," Correa said. "We don't have a guy who's going to mess with that team chemistry. Last year, the chemistry was not that great. We didn't have a leader to lead us on the right path. This year we have two. We have Beltran and we have [Brian] McCann leading us on the right path."

The first crack did not appear until May 21. After dropping two of three games to the defending American League champion Indians in late April, the Astros were swept by Cleveland in a three-game series that saw 104,620 fans show up at Minute Maid Park to watch the best team in baseball. The Astros were outscored 16–9 overall by the Indians, though, and faced adversity for the first time since they left Florida.

They were obviously good. But could they be great? And now they would be playing without two key names. Keuchel was placed on the 10-day disabled list due to a pinched nerve in his neck, while McCann was on the seven-day DL after suffering a concussion. "The ebbs and flows of the season are difficult," said Hinch, after Cleveland put up eight runs before the fifth inning in the series finale, silencing 33,476 in the stands. "You try to stay as even-keeled as you can. But we had a rough weekend—that's the bottom line. They did a better job of playing the game, and that's why they're a good team as well. We'll bounce back from this."

Joe Musgrove's ERA had ballooned to 5.63 after the second-year right-hander gave up eight hits and seven runs in three-plus innings to Cleveland. With Mike Fiers unpredictable and holding a 5.14 ERA, questions that shadowed the Astros throughout spring training—Keuchel's health, the overall strength of the rotation—reappeared.

"To be honest with you, the Indians outplayed us in just about every area," Hinch said. "They did a really good job this series, and that's why they came away with the wins."

The Astros were still 29–15. But for the first time all year, it felt like their season could go sideways or backward. Could they right themselves and avoid a slide? The veteran leadership that Correa mentioned at the start of the series stood out after the sweep. "We have to," Beltran said. "That's the mentality. You have to let go what is already in the past and move on to the next series."

The Astros did exactly what Beltran advised. They won 13 of their next 14 games—including 11 consecutive victories from May 25 to June 5—taking three of four from the Detroit Tigers, then sweeping the Baltimore Orioles, Minnesota Twins, and the once-intimidating Texas Rangers. By June 5, the best team in baseball was stronger and hotter than ever: 42–16, with a 14-game American League West lead in a division race that was already over.

All those losses from 2011 to 2014 were a long time ago.

Keuchel guided the Astros through the initial two months of the 2017 season, reaching 9–0 on June 2 and posting a stingy 1.67 ERA. One of the best pitchers in 2015 was back. And every time the thickly bearded lefthander from Oklahoma took the mound, his team believed it was staring at another win before the first pitch. When the Astros hit the 40-win mark, Keuchel possessed the most victories, lowest ERA, and second-best WHIP, BAA, and OPS in the sport. He was named AL Pitcher of the Month in April, added three more victories in four May starts, and did not suffer his first defeat of 2017 until August 2.

A neverending collection of names would carry the Astros during their World Series year. The first was Keuchel, who had also carried the team to the playoffs in 2015. "We need Keuchel and McCullers to get back to the form that we know they can deliver when they're at their best," general manager Jeff Luhnow said. Keuchel fought through a neck issue in May. But he was limited again in June and eventually returned to the disabled list for an extended stay, just as the Astros were reaching their first peak of 2017. Keuchel only made two starts in June and July, forcing baseball's best team to extend its rotation just as the season was heating up.

Enter Brad Peacock.

There were unlikely season savers. Then there was Peacock, who made 24 starts for the 92-loss Astros in 2014 and finished the 2016 season strong, but was a long shot to even make the 2017 Opening Day roster when the Astros first arrived in West Palm Beach. The 29-year-old right-hander earned the win during Springer's 13th-inning walk-off against Seattle on April 5, finished the first month of the season by allowing just one run and four hits in eight games and 11⅓ total innings of relief, then made his first start of 2017 on May 22 against Detroit. Peacock's 4⅓ innings of one-hit, eight-strikeout ball against the Tigers at Minute Maid Park set the tone for a season that just kept becoming a better story with each passing month.

Peacock was inserted into Hinch's starting rotation for a one-start replacement, following Keuchel's first trip to the DL. By the end of the regular season, Peacock would start 21 games and pitch in 34, finishing what was by far the best year of his career with a 13–2 mark, 3.00 ERA, 1.189 WHIP, and 161 strikeouts in 132 innings. "The ones who had to grind—the ones who actually went through it—you kind of respect it and pull for those guys who had to get it the hard way," said reliever Tony Sipp, who was one of many Astros pulling for Peacock when he received his initial spot start.

In 2013 Peacock began his first season with the rebuilding Astros as the No. 4 starter on what became the worst team in franchise history. Four years later, Hinch walked up the dugout steps, crossed from red dirt to green grass and gradually made his way toward the Minute Maid Park mound. Peacock had delivered in Keuchel's absence, setting up a next-man-up rotation that would eventually carry the Astros to Game 7 of the World Series. "I wanted to tell him I was proud of him," Hinch said. "I wanted to say that, 'Look, everything that we asked, you stepped up and did.'"

Peacock's father, Jerry, also beamed with pride. He had followed his son's bouncing path for years. Jerry had a heavily worn "lucky shirt" to prove it—tattered and wrinkled, mostly white, with colored fish moving in a variety of directions—and had a proud habit of catching his son's final bullpen warmup ball and adding the family souvenir to an ever-growing collection. When Peacock pitched, his father almost always was there. "You should have seen him follow me around in the minor leagues," Peacock said. "He had a closed-in lawnmower trailer that he put an air-conditioning unit in and a mattress....I'd be like, 'Dad, you could stay in my apartment.' And he wouldn't do it."

When Peacock made his strong fill-in start May 22, setting up an unexpected run that would help carry the Astros to Game 7 against the Los Angeles Dodgers, his father watched it all with proud eyes. Starter, reliever, minor leaguer, long reliever, spot starter—Peacock had literally done it all. In 2017 he would become one of the most valuable arms for a world champion.

"I was waiting [near the dugout] when he came out, but he didn't show up. He usually comes out 30 minutes before," said Jerry, describing the pregame bullpen ritual. "I wasn't sure what was going on, so I started to pack up. Then he came out. And I've got this traditional whistle I do. When I whistle, he goes looking. He'll turn that head like a rooster, looking around until he finds me."

Heart—the softer, warmer side of the Astros—was an increasingly critical component of the team. The beat only became stronger in 2017.

Since 2011, Altuve had seen almost everything the game had to offer. A slow, massive rebuilding project and 100-loss seasons. Minute Maid Park reborn during the playoffs. Batting titles, All-Star Games, Silver Slugger awards, and a Gold Glove. Then Altuve became a father. The Astros second baseman's eyes lit up when discussing his new world with his baby girl.

"To have my first daughter is life-changing, and it seems like you have a new purpose to go out there and do everything you do," Altuve said. "It's different. I would like to describe how it is, but it is difficult. Before, you always had a purpose to help your team. But now it feels like everything you do is for her first and then for the rest of the people. It's great. I love my daughter, and I hope to be a good dad."

Family life had become a key part of the Astros under Hinch, who was also a husband with two daughters. Players were regularly seen with their children at Minute Maid Park after games. Since he had taken over the team, the manager had maintained an "open clubhouse," where family was welcome and star athletes were allowed to be fathers away from home.

"You miss a lot as a dad with the schedule," said Hinch, whose father, Dennis, had died at 39 from a heart attack. "We also get a huge benefit of having a few months off at a time, too. So you try to focus on the positives. You try to provide for your kids and show them, to be honest with you, things in this life I never would have dreamed of being able to show them. There's huge upside in what we do. There's also some moments that you miss that you can't get back." He added, "If you can't share this with your kids, who can you share it with? The sons and daughters will always be welcome while I'm the manager here."

McCann had struggled with missing out on things when he first became a dad. McCann would fall asleep in the early morning after winding down from another late-night game, then always be on the verge of another road trip during a season that never seemed to end. "Early on, it was really hard. You're trying to find that balance of newborns waking up in the morning," said the veteran catcher who was already locked in with and being praised by the Astros' staff. "You feel like you should be waking up, but you're not going to sleep until 1:00 or 2:00 in the morning, and then you get up and play a game that night."

During the initial run of the best season of his career, Altuve was still adjusting. When the Astros were at home, the hours between 9:00 AM and when he left for work at Minute Maid Park were precious. "I try to keep it balanced. I want to have a personality outside of baseball," Altuve said. "I forget everything about baseball when I get home. I try to spend time with my wife and my daughter. That's a good therapy for baseball, especially when you go 0-for-4. You go home, and you truly forget about everything, and you come here the next day just fresh in your mind and try to have a good game."

As McCann's kids grew older, the balance between fatherhood and baseball began to make more sense. "You only get to play baseball for so long, so you need to get everything out of it that you can," McCann said. "But I think about it all the time: taking my kids to school every day, being there 24/7."

Already known for a strong clubhouse, the 2017 Astros only became tighter. They had also remained mostly injury-free during April. But by May, Charlie Morton, Musgrove, Keuchel, and McCann would spend time on the DL. June then saw the Astros lose Reddick, McCullers, and Keuchel again, while Will Harris, Springer, and Correa—who missed six weeks due to a torn ligament in his left thumb—were sidelined in July. Which, of course, was the same month that the best hitter in baseball unleashed the best month of his career.

April and May belonged to Keuchel. July was all Altuve, who batted a ridiculous .485, slugged .727, posted a .523 OBP, racked up 48 hits, clubbed four home runs, and recorded 21 RBIs in a single month. There was hot. Then there was Altuve scorching in July.

The Astros went 16–9 in April, 22–7 in May, 16–11 in June, and 15–9 in July. Altuve was hitting .347 by the All-Star break and went 3-for-4 with a homer, three RBIs, and four runs during the

Astros' 19–1 beatdown of Toronto that preceded the Midsummer Classic.

On July 11, Altuve was the AL's starting second baseman and one of MLB's top vote-getters in the annual All-Star Game. With the Astros second to only the Dodgers in World Series predictions, Altuve was finally getting the international recognition he had long deserved.

"The thing about him that's so impressive is that he won the batting title last year and he told Beltran when they [first] went out to eat, 'How do I get better?'" Springer said. "It's hard to tell somebody who just led all of [the league] in hitting how you get better. His desire to get better and his desire to improve in all aspects of his game...he's a team player. He wants to be successful for the team, and it's not ever about him. It's impressive and it's very, very honorable and very admirable as a teammate to see him do what he does."

Altuve studied three modern hitters the most: Miguel Cabrera, Mike Trout, and Robinson Cano. As his plate approach evolved at the major league level, the Venezuela native added aspects of Cabrera's inside-out attack and power to all fields. "It's the mindset of getting on base. It doesn't matter how I get it....It's always going to feel good," said Altuve, who didn't reach .300 until his fourth season in the majors and was viewed by the Astros as a long-term question mark at the plate early in his career. Altuve was never even supposed to make it to the show. But one of the biggest bargains in modern baseball always believed in himself and his future in MLB.

"It's going to sound crazy. But since I signed with the Astros, I knew that I just needed an opportunity to be up here," said Altuve, who signed with the franchise in 2006 as an undrafted free agent out of Venezuela for a $15,000 bonus. "I didn't know that I was going to be hitting .365...and I got a couple batting titles. But I always knew that I was going to be able to play hard. And I'm a firm believer that when you play hard, good things are going to be happening."

Altuve was initially a good but limited player—free swinging, erratic plate discipline—on a horrible team. By 2014, he had won his first batting title (.341) on the 70–92 Astros and began to display the all-around evolution that later captured his game. Three seasons after his first hitting crown, Altuve entered August 2017 rivaling New York Yankees rookie slugger Aaron Judge as the leading candidate for AL MVP and had become the face of the Astros on a team loaded with young, highly likeable stars.

Altuve was a true must-see—an old-school throwback worth paying big money to sit as close as possible for. He played the sport daily with child-like joy, took pride in being covered in dirt and consistently signed autographs for pleading fans.

"Altuve! Altuve! Altuve!!!" kids called out, begging for simple recognition and lasting proof of greatness.

As he made his way to the plate once again, Altuve was adamant that his primary thought always revolved around finding some way to get on base. But much of his success was also due to pre- and in-game preparation. "It's a combination," Altuve said. "Sometimes you have to believe in your instincts and what you think they're going to do to you. But sometimes you really have to follow what the coaches say. It's really hard to pick: should I go with my instincts or should I go with [the advice]? I don't know if it's 50-50, but it just depends."

In early August, the Astros were on the verge of their 70th win of the season and playing Tampa Bay during a three-game homestand at Minute Maid Park. A 3–1 lead turned into 5–3 Rays in the seventh, sending fans streaming into the hot Houston night. Correa and Springer were missing. The Astros' bullpen was shaky, and social media was already assigning blame.

Altuve answered it all by studying the game that was still being played. He had not faced Sergio Romo in a while, but knew the

10th-year right-handed reliever relied on a slider. How large was the sweep and how often was the veteran still turning to the pitch in 2017? Video rolled as Altuve's eyes locked in before the bottom of the seventh arrived. "I can see what he was doing," Altuve said. "His slider is big. So I was like, 'Okay, if you pull this guy, you're not going to be able to get a hit.' So I was trying to hit the ball to right field."

A.J. Reed struck out. Jake Marisnick grounded out. The stadium was half empty as Romo went up 0–1 on Altuve via an 85-mph fastball. A low-and-away slider followed and missed. The third pitch was almost the same and out of the strike zone, but a little closer to the plate and within Altuve's reach. He stretched his body outward, extended his hands and arms, and made classic Altuve contact. Romo's 75-mph slider became a soft liner that ended up in the outfield. "I was trying to hit the ball to right field and I still hit it to center field because of the good spin he has on the slider," Altuve said.

He was not done. Altuve's 151st hit of 2017 soon had him standing on third base after Bregman singled and Altuve stole third. The best player on the best team in the AL did not make it home in the seventh inning of game 108. But Altuve's daily devotion was impossible to ignore, even during a rare three-game losing streak.

"He feels like he can get better every year," Beltran said. "That's a great mentality to have in this game. This game, you've got to stay humble. No matter how well you do, you've got to be humble."

July was as close to perfect as possible for Altuve. By the first day of the fifth month of the season, the Astros led the AL West by 15 games. And on July 30, the deep connecting lines of a potential storybook season became even stronger when Bagwell joined longtime teammate Biggio in the National Baseball Hall of Fame. Orange was the primary color in Cooperstown, New York, as longtime Astros believers—proudly wearing Altuve, Correa, Bagwell, and

Biggio jerseys—converged and reunited in baseball heaven, during a season that had felt special since February.

"I want to thank the Astros fans. You guys have been absolutely wonderful," Bagwell said during his induction speech. "I can't tell you how much being around you guys in the city and showing me the love and my family—this is where my kids were born, this is where my kids were raised. I love you so much for everything that you've done for me."

A brilliant beginning by Keuchel (9–0, 1.67 ERA) and a sharp start for McCullers (6–1, 2.58) fell in line with everything that went so right for the Astros when 2017 began. The bats rarely wavered, Morton and Peacock made up for Collin McHugh's absence, and the Astros placed a team record six players in the All-Star Game: Altuve, Correa, Springer, Keuchel, McCullers, and Chris Devenski.

Biggio had been around the Astros regularly, spending time with the team during batting practice and interacting with everyone who crossed his path. Bagwell watched the best team in the American League nightly, pulled in by the Astros' young names and their dedication to the game. "I've watched more baseball since I retired than I ever have in my life," Bagwell said. "Watching them every single night is just so much fun. You never can turn the TV off. They have so much talent—and young talent."

Twelve years after Bagwell appeared in the 2005 Fall Classic with the Astros, Houston's daily obsession with wins and losses had returned. "The city has really taken in this team," he said. "Everywhere I go, even when they lose, people will say, 'Wow, what happened last night?' I say, 'Well, hey, man, they're not going to win every game.'"

Marwin González could have been the Astros' seventh All-Star in Miami. He spent the first half of the season as the team's most underrated player, then stayed home during the break and spent time with his family in Houston.

By the 90th game of the season, González was more comfortable than ever playing wherever the Astros needed him—holding down left field, hitting eighth in Hinch's loaded lineup—and had evolved into one of the best utility men in the sport. He was hitting .308 with 16 home runs, 53 RBIs, and a .967 OPS, then went 3-for-5 with another homer and two more RBIs. "He was the MVP of the first half for us," Correa said. "Not only his offensive numbers, just the fact that he plays every position—he's so valuable. That's what 'valuable player' means to me, and he's been the most valuable asset in our clubhouse."

First base, second, shortstop, or third—it did not matter. The 28-year-old from Venezuela had become as valuable as it gets for a manager who used 75 batting orders before the All-Star Game. Hinch referred to González as the Astros' "Swiss Army Knife" and had never been more proud of the do-everything, team-first athlete.

"He's been incredibly important....His actual production has been incredible," Hinch said. "And his growth as a hitter has allowed me to do a lot of different things."

González's pro career began at 17 in 2006 in the Chicago Cubs organization. After being a fill-in player with the 100-plus loss 2012 and 2013 Astros—González spent 57 combined games in Triple A during those rebuilding seasons—his major league games played increased from 103 in 2014 to 141 in 2016.

With three months left in his 2017 campaign, González already had career highs in homers and RBIs, while his batting average was 54 points higher than last year's mark and his OPS had increased by a whopping .273. "I want to finish it strong," González said. "That's the main goal. It's not how you start, it's how you finish."

The Astros' roll finally stopped as the fifth month of the regular season approached. The questions from West Palm Beach returned in August. And Hinch's club stumbled through its first losing month of the season, only playing .393 ball and dropping 17 of 28 games.

Keuchel joined McHugh on the disabled list, Morton was injured, and Musgrove and McCullers also appeared on the DL, leaving Fiers (4–2, 4.29 ERA) at one point as the most dependable starting arm on a World Series contender. As the July 31 non-waiver trade deadline had drawn closer, the line, "We need some pitching," was privately issued at Minute Maid Park.

Cleveland was only 57–47 on August 1, but the defending AL champs were about to run through a 19–9 month, then roll off 22 consecutive wins for a 25–4 September. The Dodgers won at least 19 games each month from May through July, entering August five wins better than Houston. The Astros had not made a major deadline move since 2015, when Luhnow sent four prospects to Milwaukee in exchange for outfielder Carlos Gomez and Fiers. Fiers had thrown a no-hitter that August but spent 2017 on the edge of the Astros' rotation. Gomez was released in August 2016 after hitting just .221 with nine home runs and a .619 OPS in 126 games for the Astros.

After a disappointing 2016 trade deadline, the questions were heard louder than ever. Years had been devoted to a massive rebuilding that tore the franchise down to its core. Now that the Astros had something special on the big-league field, was the front office going to back its major league team during a critical point in a highly promising season? And was Luhnow willing to trade away more prospects—the gamble had not worked in 2015—for a single high-priced veteran who might allow the Astros to compete with MLB's elite in September and October?

Fans, media, and anyone who had watched and studied the Astros' rise were divided as the July 31 non-waiver deadline approached. It was "go for it" versus "save it for later." The new regime had always said that it was building for the long term and the Astros' championship window had just opened. But Luhnow was also in his sixth season as GM and the farthest his reconstructed team had been thus far was an AL Division Series collapse against the eventual World Series champion Royals in 2015. Those Astros had been good. But their season-long limitations had let them down in mid-October. The 2017 Astros, maybe, could be great.

Altuve was having an MVP year, Correa and Springer had been midseason candidates before injuries, and a loaded 1–9 lineup had set records since April. Keuchel had been a Cy Young Award favorite in the early months, while everyone from González and Marisnick to Peacock and Morton had helped push the Astros to their best start in team history. As August approached, though, Hinch's club was stretched thin for the first time all year and hoping for an external lift.

The division had been locked up by June. They already had 69 wins on July 31. But if the Astros were going to reach a stage only one other team in franchise history had ever seen, they needed more support from a front office that had been moving around names and constructing an annual contender for years.

The playoff heat of October was just two months away. There was no way the Astros were going to allow the Dodgers, Yankees, Cubs, Nationals, and the rest of baseball's best teams to make significant improvements before the deadline, while they simply asked their as-is roster to do more. Right?

10

IT WILL BRING HOPE

Hello, Houston. It's good to be home. I want to start out by thanking all of you by being here. A very special day for us to start the rebuild process of our great city....We wear this patch on our jersey the rest of the year to represent you. So stay strong. Be strong. And we appreciate every one of you.

—A.J. Hinch

FOR ONE MONTH, it felt like everything was falling apart. Their year. Their season. Then their city.

A.J. Hinch's Astros only had one losing month in 2017. After a 15–9 July, which featured six Astros in the All-Star Game and MVP candidate José Altuve hitting .485, a team that spent the early part of the season as the best club in baseball grinded through an 11–17 August and showed its first signs of fraying.

After another quiet non-waiver trade deadline had passed in Houston, the Cy Young Award winner who had carried the 2015 team and first sparked the 2017 squad spoke up. It had been a while since anyone had publicly called out the Astros' front office. Dallas Keuchel stood inside the Astros' clubhouse the day after the deadline and made his voice heard. "I'm not going to lie. Disappointment is a little bit of an understatement," said Keuchel, who debuted with the Astros in 2012 and had endured two 100-plus-loss seasons. "I felt like a bunch of teams really bolstered their roster for the long haul and for a huge playoff push, and us just kind of staying pat was really disappointing to myself."

The Astros faced a divide. They were a good team that could be great—with the right additions. The rotation had already been extended, the bullpen could only hold on for so long, and the only nightly guarantee was that the bats could always come through. The staff clearly needed another big-name arm if the franchise was going to hold its own during the playoffs with baseball's best teams. And whether it was veterans who had signed on with the belief that 2017 could be something special in Houston or former role players such as Marwin González who were now in the middle of career years, the team's decision makers owed it to the players on the field. The club had done its part. The front office needed to hold up its end of the bargain.

The mounting complexities of the trade deadline had tied the Astros' hands. General manager Jeff Luhnow acknowledged disappointment after veteran lefthander Francisco Liriano was the team's only move on July 31. An outside—and, at times, inside—belief was reinforced: the Astros still were not fully committed to doing everything they could to win their first World Series and were still prizing young prospects and the promise of the future over the present day. Lingering issues that dated back to an abysmal 51–111 season in 2013 were still being felt.

"Good teams can always be great and great teams can be legendary. At the end of the year, you want to be the only ones left, and it is a little disappointing, for sure," said Keuchel, who threw for 2012–2013 Astros teams that lost a combined 218 games.

By 2017 Keuchel was one of the longest-tenured veterans left from the horrible rebuilding seasons, had as much personal drive as anyone on the roster, and had spent six years in Houston waiting for his team to take the next step. The Astros still had not done it.

"I'd be lying if I didn't say I was disappointed in not getting some of the moves done that we were working on," Luhnow said. "We had some that were close to and almost over the finish line, and at times I would put them at 90 percent–plus that we were going to get them done."

The Astros were still 69–36. But a deadline that was always about extra pitching had seen relievers Tony Sipp and Michael Feliz join Will Harris on the disabled list, a day after starter Lance McCullers Jr. was sidelined again. The worn-down bullpen held a 4.53 ERA, which was tied for 23rd with the distant Rangers and would not cut it in the playoffs.

"I know a lot of the guys feel like we can win in here, and that's a pretty accurate statement, and that is why we have built such a great lead," Keuchel said. "When it comes down to it, we're going to win for each other, and that's it."

The honesty from an outspoken lefthander was soon backed by an unorthodox outfielder. Keuchel was not the only Astro who spoke up. "Deep down, everybody in that clubhouse knew we were going to make some move to turn us from a really great team to a team that would put us over the edge, especially with all the moves you saw around the league," Josh Reddick told MLB Network Radio. "It's nothing against our guys, but any time you can make your team better you should have the opportunity to do that and take full advantage. I think deep down we were all down in the dumps because we had a pretty good shot to help this team get over the hump to where we need to be. That time has passed, and we can't dwell on that. We have all the confidence in everybody we have now, we just have to get out of this slump."

The summer slump only continued.

The Astros recorded their longest losing streak of the season from August 8 to 12, dropping five consecutive games to the Chicago White Sox and Texas Rangers. After opening the month with three straight home defeats to Tampa Bay, Hinch's team dropped series at Minute Maid Park to the Washington Nationals and the Rangers, while the lineup struggled for the first time all season. After hitting .294 in June and .323 in July with 90 combined homers during the two months, the Astros' average dropped to .254 in August with a season-low .726 OPS. The pitching kept falling backward, too: a 3.38 team ERA in April had jumped to 4.79 in June and 5.08 by July. The monthly ERA improved to 4.00 in August, but opponents recorded their second-highest monthly OPS (.748) all season.

In mid-August, the Astros had gone 11–15 since the All-Star break and allowed the surging Boston Red Sox to pull within just five games of the best overall mark in the American League with 46 contests to go. Injuries were also piling up. For the initial two months of the 2017 season, the Astros were the best team in baseball and relatively worry-free. When someone briefly went down (Brian McCann, Jake Marisnick, Keuchel), someone else immediately stepped into an increased role (Evan Gattis, Brad Peacock, González). Carlos Correa, George Springer, Keuchel, and McCullers were all added to the DL, though, and Hinch had used 100 different batting orders in 115 games, with untested names such as Derek Fisher, J.D. Davis, and Tyler White called on to fill out the August holes. It was starting to feel like the end of 2016 again.

"I want to get our team back," said Hinch, whose club dropped 12 of 16 games from July 29 to August 14. Which was just about the time that Justin Verlander's name began to be publicly reattached to the team that had not done anything significant at the first trade deadline.

That whiff hurt so bad because the Astros—Keuchel, Reddick, the front office, fans…everyone—knew exactly what the team needed since July 2016. In the summer of 2017, the Los Angeles Dodgers and New York Yankees added big-name starters. The Astros had not. And when Keuchel returned to the mound July 28 after a nearly two-month layoff, the pitcher who had started the season 9–0 initially was not the same.

"We'll clean it up and I need to be better. It all started with me…. It wasn't a very good game by any means," said Keuchel, who went 2–3 in August with a 5.05 ERA, allowing 35 hits in 35⅔ innings.

By mid-August, the Astros clearly needed a jolt and were consistently linked in national trade rumors to a 34-year-old Detroit right-hander who had once been one of the premier arms in the game. But the feeling lingered that Verlander would continue to be a Tiger in 2017, while the as-is Astros would have to rely on themselves as the final month of the regular season approached.

Los Angeles outfielder Yasiel Puig proclaimed that his team would be in the World Series after a walkoff double had propelled the Dodgers to a surreal 85–34 record. The Astros were salvaging a 2–6 road trip with Max Stassi, Peacock, and Davis, still trying to prove to the rest of baseball that they were not going to be undone by an internal letdown at the deadline.

They dropped four of six from August 20 to 26 against the Oakland Athletics, Nationals, and Los Angeles Angels, with only Mike Fiers and Collin McHugh—who did not make his first start of 2017 until July 22—picking up wins.

Then the storm hit.

It came out of nowhere, was mostly ignored at first and did not start forever changing lives in America's fourth-largest city until the end of the week. Once the nonstop rain finally ended and Hurricane Harvey's destruction was complete, Houston would endure the greatest natural disaster in the city's history, and the Astros—the season, the team, the fan base—would never be the same.

"I hope all your families are safe," quarterback Tom Savage said late in the evening of August 26, after the Texans were shut out by the New Orleans Saints in an NFL preseason game. They were the last words Savage issued before walking out of a small postgame press-conference room at the Superdome. As the Texans were packing up inside a lasting landmark from Hurricane Katrina's destruction in 2005—lasting proof that proud people can always rebuild the cities they call home—Hurricane Harvey was starting to soak Houston.

"Mother Nature is undefeated," said Texans coach Bill O'Brien, whose team was about to fly to Dallas as a temporary home. Four days prior, the Texans had flown to New Orleans as a tropical depression in the Gulf of Mexico first began to draw attention. On August 25, a Category 4 hurricane slammed Texas' southern coast. Two days later, Houston was the televised center of the nation and words like "catastrophic" had become commonplace when describing Harvey's impact on the city and nearby regions.

"Local rainfall amounts of 50 inches would exceed any previous Texas rainfall record. The breadth and intensity of this rainfall are beyond anything experienced before," the National Weather Service tweeted.

The Astros were stuck in Anaheim, California. Then Dallas. Then Harvey kept pouring, Houston kept flooding, and a three-game homestand against the Rangers at Minute Maid Park was relocated to the Tampa Bay Rays' stadium in St. Petersburg, Florida. The Astros dropped two of three games to Texas before minor league–like crowds of 3,485 on August 29; 6,123 on August 30; and 3,385 on August 31. In the days before the final trade deadline of the 2017 season—players could still be acquired, but deals were rare and names had to pass through waivers—Hinch's club was separated from its home, while right field at Minute Maid Park was under water and Houston was beginning the long, slow recovery from the most devastating hurricane the city had ever faced.

Houston needed help.

Texans defensive end J.J. Watt turned an impromptu personal message to his millions of social-media followers into a grassroots flood-relief fund, eventually raising more than $37 million and being named the NFL's Walter Payton Man of the Year for his efforts. Houston Rockets guard James Harden tweeted a photo of a rain-covered Texas with "PRAY" in the middle. Chris Paul echoed his new teammate: "My heart and prayers are with you Texas!" As the Astros began a "home" series about 1,000 miles away from home—the

Rangers had declined a proposal to play the series in Arlington, Texas; it was just the fourth time in MLB history that games were relocated to a neutral site because of weather—interstates and streets in Houston were covered in water, houses and entire neighborhoods were flooded, two major airports were silenced, and photos, videos, and nationally televised pleas just kept coming.

One of the simplest but strongest messages came from a baseball team: "For Houston. #PlayBall."

But when would the Astros return to their flooded city?

Staring at the potential of 19 consecutive road games—a 10-game West Coast road trip followed a scheduled three-game homestand against the New York Mets—the Astros were leaning closer toward extending their stay in St. Petersburg and following up their relocated series against the Rangers by "hosting" New York. Then two intertwined, season-changing decisions were made at almost the same time. On August 30, a strong push from Houston Mayor Sylvester Turner led to an announcement that the Astros would play an old-fashioned day-night doubleheader at Minute Maid Park on Saturday, September 2. "We feel that the Astros playing this weekend will provide a much-needed boost for our city," Turner said. "With all of the difficulties that many of our citizens are facing, the games will provide an opportunity for families to start returning to some aspect of normal life."

A day later, the final minutes of August 31 were devoted to a move that was a season in the making.

It had been a month since the Astros whiffed at the non-waiver trade deadline, leading to Keuchel's comment that "disappointment is a little bit of an understatement" and Reddick acknowledging his team was "down in the dumps." The day before the Astros returned to their recovering city, Luhnow pulled an all-nighter to pull off a franchise-changing deal that revived Houston and its ballclub all at once, ultimately leading to the first World Series title in franchise history.

The Astros wrapped Verlander in orange and blue—only after he approved the deal, which was held up by a no-trade clause—and shipped three prospects (Franklin Perez, Daz Cameron, Jake Rogers) to the Detroit Tigers. By finalizing the deal minutes before September 1, the 2011 AL MVP and Cy Young Award winner was eligible to take the mound for the Astros in the playoffs.

In the early hours of September 1, the realization began sinking in for a long-starved fan base and rebuilding city. Verlander was coming to Houston. The Astros suddenly had a World Series arm and world championship potential. The Astros were a long, long way from the start of their rebuild and tearing everything down. They were building upward and adding on while their city was in need.

"There's a lot of people that suffered tremendous loss over the course of the last week, and our city's going to be suffering the consequences of this storm for a long time to come," Luhnow said. "We as the Astros organization are doing everything we can to help those people in need. And part of our responsibility is to provide a distraction, entertainment, hope, aspirations for the future—all of the things that people turn to sports for. So we recognize our part in this, and we recognize our part in the healing."

At the time, the Astros were 80–53 and on the verge of giving away the best record in the AL to the Cleveland Indians, who had reached Game 7 of the World Series a year ago and were within 2¹/₂ games with 29 games to go. And even though Verlander's ERA had floated around 4.50 from April through July, the six-time All-Star had 16 playoff starts, had pitched in two World Series and was 5–2 with a 2.41 ERA since the 2017 All-Star break, striking out 78 in 67¹/₃ innings while allowing a .186 batting average.

In Astros orange, he would instantly become a must-see every time he took the mound, whether it was at Minute Maid Park or on a distant flat-screen TV. And with one of baseball's many beauties being its existence as a daily pastime, watching and keeping up with the Astros and Verlander during Houston's post-Harvey recovery was about to become the highlight of so many otherwise frustrating days.

"It'll bring hope, something to look forward to, while we rebuild the city and rebuild parts of the city that some of us can't fathom that have been destroyed," said Hinch, discussing his club's return to Houston. "We are a baseball team. We will keep it in proper perspective. We provide entertainment and escape for a lot of people in our community. Whether it's the guys that have been here all year or the new additions, I think this team will work really hard to make this city proud and make this city feel good at a time where there's a lot of people who are going through some tough times."

Before the first-ever doubleheader at Minute Maid Park, the Astros spent their September 1 off-day at a Hurricane Harvey relief shelter. Charlie Morton, Chris Devenski, Collin McHugh, McCann, González, Peacock, Marisnick, Altuve, Reddick, and Hinch were among Astros who visited with evacuees, many of whom had seen their residences reduced to the smallest of living spaces inside the George R. Brown Convention Center, which had housed a key part of the NFL's Super Bowl LI experience in February and was just blocks away from the Astros' downtown ballpark.

Altuve danced with an evacuee as González watched nearby. Astros relievers filled in as Houstonians just beginning to piece their lives back together collected simple items from a supply line. Hinch made the rounds, listening to stories and sharing smiles with Astros fans relieved to see familiar faces up close.

For as long as the rest of their 2017 season lasted, the Astros now had two goals: win a world championship and lift up a city that needed them more than ever. "Having a team that is on its way to hopefully a successful September and a long postseason run will give people in Houston a healthy distraction and something to think about other than all the loss around them," Luhnow said. "We're hoping that Justin Verlander is another part of that...

helping us put together a really successful end to this season to help this city."

On the first day that baseball returned to Houston after the destruction and horror of Harvey, the lines began forming while the sun was still rising and the ballpark was just returning to life. Parents and children. Fathers and sons. Married couples. Many swapping storm stories as the Astros took two from the Mets, 12–8 and 4–1, before a combined crowd of 65,223 at Minute Maid Park. Hinch's team knocked Matt Harvey out of the first game, recording eight hits and seven runs before the third inning even arrived, then began a six-game winning streak that set the tone for the rest of their season.

Energy. Passion. Perseverance.

Altuve jerseys, Correa shirts, and orange and blue hats were everywhere. After Turner threw the ceremonial first pitch, Hinch held a microphone and sounded like a mayor, marking a "special day" for a rebuilding city and pushing Houston's residents to "stay strong." When Reddick, who wore a throwback "Stylin' and Pro-filin'" Ric Flair T-shirt pregame, walked to the plate, "woooos" immediately bounced around the revived ballpark. Then Altuve slid across the plate, barely touching the back of home with one hand and making it 3–0 Astros in the first. The stadium roared like it was full, even though the top section was mostly empty.

"We're going to play with a lot of emotion, and we're going to play with a lot of heart," said Springer, wearing a shirt with HOUS-TON STRONG stripped across the front. "The city's been through a lot over these last few days. This game was for the city."

During the doubleheader, in between two more victories in a season loaded with them, a new face walked into the Astros' clubhouse.

Verlander had arrived.

11

YOU DON'T EVEN KNOW, MAN

It's the playoffs. It's a big deal. It's fun. It's what you play for, and nobody wants to mess it up. We're going to embrace that emotion. We're going to enjoy that emotion and soak it up. Because, like I told our team after we won [the AL West], this might be the best team we are ever on. And if we don't take advantage of that emotionally or even with the opportunity we have, we'll have regret.

—A.J. Hinch

THEY WON THEIR initial six games after he became one of them. They went 20–8 in September, then collected win No. 101 on the final day of the regular season. He was instantly accepted by his teammates and fully embraced by his new city. And that still does not capture the impact that Justin Verlander had on the 2017 Astros.

He was the one they were waiting for. And once he finally arrived, he was better than they ever imagined. The first start was September 5, three days after baseball returned to Houston following the destruction of Hurricane Harvey. Verlander and the Astros in the Pacific Northwest. Six innings, six hits, one earned run, seven strikeouts, one walk, and a victory on 103 pitches (73 strikes). Verlander improved to 11–8 in 2017, lowered his ERA to 3.74, and ignited a run that only stopped because MLB ran out of games and someone had to have a parade.

He went 5–0 in September with a 1.06 ERA, striking out 43 in 34 innings and holding hitters to a .149 average. Inevitable comparisons to Randy Johnson with the 1998 Astros (10–1 with a 1.28 ERA after being traded on July 31) followed, but Verlander eventually blew past that connection and created his own world. He was a throwback in the modern era. He instantly became the Astros' new ace—deepening the rotation and giving manager A.J. Hinch more pieces to move around—and did not come off the mound until he was forced to. Just like a famous old Astro who now watched the 2017 club from behind home plate.

When Nolan Ryan was a young boy, a Dodgers power lefty caught his eye. "To this day, I'm still a Sandy [Koufax] fan. I just really thought he was one of the top three or four dominating pitchers I ever saw," said Ryan, who once made a trip to see Koufax pitch in person.

As his victories (324) and strikeouts (an MLB-record 5,714) stacked up, Ryan realized that future ballplayers were drawing inspiration from his artistry, just like he once did from Koufax. "You never know who may associate themselves in a sense with you," Ryan said. "And I always felt like if you had the opportunity to be an influence on somebody, you wanted to be a positive influence."

A young Verlander was watching. He would not sit in front of a television, stare at the set for hours, and marvel at the wonder of a baseball game—Verlander was too active and had too much energy as a child. But when a flame-throwing right-hander from Alvin, Texas, appeared on the screen, Verlander was hooked. It could be a live cut-in as another no-hitter approached or grainy ESPN Classic footage. Ryan was Verlander's guy, and Verlander was glued to the screen. "I wish I could tell you what drew me to him," Verlander said. "I'm assuming people were drawn to him because of the power and all that. But I guess his mentality on the mound and everything that came with it is kind of what I've tried to bring into my career."

Ryan threw a career-high 332⅔ innings with the California Angels in 1974, six seasons before he became an Astro. The Ryan

Express broke 300 innings twice and reached the 200-inning mark 14 times. Verlander threw a career-high 251 innings during his AL Cy Young Award/MVP season with the Detroit Tigers in 2011 and reached the 200-inning mark 10 times during his initial 13 seasons in the majors. In an era dominated by overthought bullpen specialization and starters yanked at the first sign of trouble, Ryan and Verlander believed that the first pitcher to take the ball should always fight to finish—and win—the game.

"The way they use starting pitching and the bullpen nowadays, a lot of those starters miss out on opportunities to win ballgames. In my day, they paid you on innings pitched and they paid you on wins and losses," said Ryan, who now served as executive advisor for the Astros and was regularly seen at home games.

The No. 2 overall pick of the 2004 MLB amateur draft caught Ryan's eye early in his career. Verlander threw with power, precision, and constantly attacked the plate. After he recorded his first MLB no-hitter—June 12, 2007, in a 12-strikeout home victory over Milwaukee—Verlander answered a phone and was congratulated by an unmistakable voice. "I hung up, and I didn't even remember the conversation. I don't even think I asked him anything. I was just like, 'Oh, Mr. Ryan,'" said Verlander, who also noticed Ryan watching him from the stands during the latter's front-office days with the Texas Rangers.

By late September, Astros fans were constantly calling out Verlander's name. His new team won nine of 11 games from September 12 to 23, with the 34-year-old power right-hander from Virginia collecting three of the victories. The bats returned—after a tough August, the Astros hit .271 with 34 home runs and a .793 OPS during the final month of the regular season—while the staff significantly lowered opponents' batting average and on-base percentage in September. Dallas Keuchel faced less pressure every five days and Lance McCullers Jr. was given more leeway during his return, while the bullpen would eventually benefit from extra arms that could be moved around once Verlander was added to the staff.

Verlander ultimately had to make the decision to join the Astros at the last minute. But the Cy Young Award winner who had carried the Astros to the 2015 playoffs also played a key role in guiding the longtime Tiger to Houston, just in time for the 2017 postseason. As Astros general manager Jeff Luhnow pulled the deal together at a family dining table in California, Keuchel called Verlander to make a final pitch.

"I was in the middle of a whirlwind night, and to have [Keuchel] reach out, and I was actually—I have actually apologized to him since—I was pretty quick off the phone because I told him, I said, 'Dallas, I thank you so much for the phone call, but I've got a lot of other calls I need to make right now and talk to my family and stuff,'" Verlander said. "And he completely understood. He said, 'But before you go, just one last thing.' He goes, 'You won't regret this decision if you decide to join the Houston Astros.' And that kind of resonated with me and that stuck with me. And he was one of the first calls I made after I made the deal and waived my no-trade clause and agreed to come here. I called him and let him know that I was coming to join the Astros and that his call meant a lot to me."

Once Verlander signed off, his bond with Keuchel, the rest of the staff, and a city in recovery only deepened. After a disappointing 2016 season, the Astros knew they had to add veterans to a young clubhouse that was missing playoff-proven leadership. After adding Brian McCann, Josh Reddick, and Carlos Beltran before the team arrived for spring training in West Palm Beach, Florida, Verlander gave the staff a legitimacy that was essential for October baseball.

"What makes him great already and in the clubhouse is just his mindset, the way his mind works," Keuchel said. "And I feel like my mind is unique in the way I feel about pitching and my game plan and strategy, but with his mindset, it's very similar. So we might have polar pitching tendencies, but the way our minds work is very similar. So I've bounced hundreds of questions off him already, and he would probably say the same thing. And it's just been a joy to kind of talk pitching in the dugout, especially for the younger starters. I think Lance has really benefited from him being here too, and just the pitching staff overall. He is really that ultra-veteran guy who has done everything besides win a World Series. So that was one of the things that appealed to him before he came over here."

Even with Verlander in Astros orange, the path ahead was never easy or predictable. Hurricane Harvey had devastated Houston during the days leading up to a last-minute acquisition that forever changed Astros history. By the middle of September, an image of a car covered in floodwater was tacked up on the team's clubhouse bulletin board, while Carlos Correa was wearing cleats that featured Puerto Rico's flag. Hurricanes Harvey, Irma, and Maria all hit home for the Astros.

"There's a devastating hurricane heading toward Puerto Rico and it's going to crush the island. So, obviously, my thoughts and prayers are already over there," said Correa, who later helped bring supplies to the island. "I've got most of my family over there, so I'm really worried about that. My parents and siblings are the only ones over here, so I've got a lot of people there....I talked to everybody already. But there's not much that you can do."

Hinch was not sure who tacked the Harvey flood photo to an area normally reserved for daily lineup postings, team travel information, and general updates. But the third-year manager clearly knew what the lasting image meant: the Astros' 2017 season now represented more than just baseball. "It won't be forgotten by our team, and we won't stop helping," Hinch said. "Obviously, we were the first hurricane [area] to have to deal with it. But one after another after another—we have to make sure that people continue to help someone else."

Correa also had two flood photos attached to his locker. One captured the chaos after the storm. The other showed people carrying possessions through a flood. "Every time I look at that picture, it reminds me of how God has blessed me with the talent to play this sport, but it doesn't stop there," said Correa, who obtained his pictures during a team chapel session. "I use everything he has given me in order to help other people as well. Right now, I'm helping people in Houston....[Soon] I'm going to be helping people in Puerto Rico."

Several of his teammates had similar images taped to their lockers. For veteran reliever Tony Sipp, the flood photos were proof "the battle's not over with." "A lot of things happen," he said, "and a lot of times people still suffering can be put on the back burner....Even half a year after, it's the toughest battle, trying to get life back together."

Houston rediscovered life in its baseball team. And during a season that dated back to February in sunny West Palm Beach, the Astros reached their first peak of 2017 almost six years after an unprecedented rebuild began.

There were shouts, cheers, and joyously recorded cellphone videos that would last lifetimes. Then Verlander suddenly ran away. The Astros' new ace—perfect time, perfect place—wrapped his arms around Jim Crane and embraced the owner who had made him a Houstonian less than three weeks ago.

"I don't know if you could ask for more, for your home debut to be a chance to clinch the division. I don't know how often that's happened, but it felt pretty special," said Verlander, who struck out 10 and allowed just three hits in a 7–1 home victory against the Seattle Mariners on September 17 at Minute Maid Park. The 91st win on the season handed the American League West division title—the first for the franchise since it won the National League Central in 2001—and an instant playoff spot to the Astros.

Minute Maid Park's jumbotron glowed with "2017 AL West Division Champs." Jerseys, T-shirts, and beards were drenched. The Astros raced around the outfield, high-fiving screaming fans, after celebrating in unison in the infield. Soon Reddick was taking over the clubhouse, wearing a sleeveless T-shirt with a huge American eagle on the front and thick black goggles, while calmly holding a lit cigar in his hand. The veteran outfielder was wearing barely anything else and just kept smiling.

"It's a special feeling," Reddick said. "I don't know if you can put it into words."

Players and fans tried. Some of the biggest names on the Astros had lived through the pain of the 100-loss years and a slow rebuild that sometimes felt like it would never end. When José Altuve returned to the dugout for the final time, he was serenaded by a ringing "MVP" chant from standing fans who refused to leave.

McCann captured the feeling with one word: *magical.* "You don't get this feeling every year," he said. "You embrace this.... There's a lot of things that go into this. And I'm just so thankful that I'm a part of this team."

Club Astros cranked with blinking lights and swirling smoke. Pulsing music pounded in the background; beer and champagne showers never stopped. Ken Giles danced with no one around. McCann broke out his own moves, then the 13-year veteran catcher found a sudden partner in Verlander, who pressed his back to McCann's and began bouncing backward like a zombie.

The 2017 Astros owned the AL West and clinched their division faster than any club in franchise history. With the nearest competition 15 games back and all eyes turning toward the postseason, praise was freely passed around. Luhnow referred to Hinch as the Astros' most valuable player of 2017. Keuchel knew there was "nobody better" than Verlander if the ex-Tiger took the mound in Game 1 of the AL Division Series. And with the club's chemistry never cracking, a team that was only 31–29 since the All-Star break was believing in itself again, at the same time that post-Harvey Houston was starting to become obsessed with the Astros.

"There was really nobody better in the American League on paper [in spring training]," Keuchel said. "We just had to put it together."

Just 15 days after the Astros returned home to help their city return to normal, Hinch pulled Marwin González and Altuve into his chest, hugging two Astros who had been through so much. George Springer and Correa ended the first of many celebrations by walking across the infield and pointing at all the standing, screaming fans. And 40-year-old Carlos Beltran, once mercilessly booed at Minute Maid Park every time he returned to the plate, danced around like a kid.

"You don't even know, man. I've been here since 2013, and I've been through the rough times," Brad Peacock said.

The clubhouse plastic was ripped down. Children started running the bases, taking over the field once covered by the Astros and their families. Then the owner, who had been so warmly embraced by Verlander, said what needed to be said. If 2017 really was going to be the Astros' year, it was not even close to being over. "We want to win a World Series here and that's what we're working for," Crane said.

Baseball being baseball, questions still remained. The Cleveland Indians had just rolled off 22 consecutive wins from August 24 to September 14, then won five straight after finally losing a game. On the day the Astros clinched their division, the AL's 2016 pennant winner had two more victories than Hinch's team and was heading toward ending the long 162 with the best record in the league. The Dodgers had finally returned to earth. But Los Angeles was still an MLB-leading 96–53 on September 17 and the easy pick to win the World Series.

Verlander had given the Astros a new Game 1 ace and was only getting stronger with each start. After a 5.05 ERA in August,

Astros left-handed starter Dallas Keuchel is fired up after striking out the Yankees' Aaron Judge in Game 1 of the 2017 ALCS. Keuchel shut down New York on seven innings of four-hit, no-run ball, with 10 Ks and one walk to earn the win in a 2–1 Houston victory.

Justin Verlander delivers in the first inning of Game 6 of the 2017 ALCS. Verlander pitched seven innings of shutout ball in a 7–1 Astros win that tied the series at 3–3. Verlander was 4–1 with a 2.21 ERA in the 2017 postseason and was named the ALCS MVP.

Altuve hugs the American League Championship trophy with manager A.J. Hinch after the Astros won the pennant over the New York Yankees, shutting them out 4–0 in Game 7 of the 2017 ALCS.

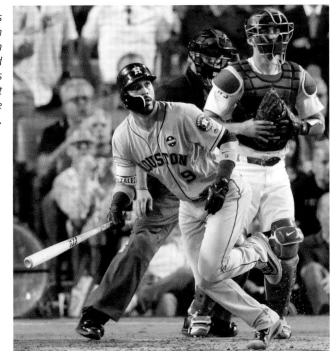

Marwin González watches his game-tying home run leave Dodger Stadium in Game 2 of the 2017 World Series against the Los Angeles Dodgers. His blast made it 3–3 in the top of the ninth inning.

Altuve hits a home run in the 10th inning of Game 2 to put the Astros ahead of the Dodgers 4–3.

After the Dodgers tied Game 2, at 5–5 in the bottom of the 10th, George Springer rounds the bases in the top of the 11th inning, having just hit a two-run, go-ahead home run. This time the two runs were enough, as the Astros held on to win it in 11 innings, 7–6.

Altuve is congratulated by Alex Bregman and Yuli Gurriel after hitting a three-run homer in the fifth inning of Game 5 of the 2017 World Series to tie it at 7–7.

Alex Bregman raises his arms after hitting the game-winner, a walk-off single to left field in the bottom of the 10th inning that scored pinch-runner Derek Fisher, giving the Astros a 13–12 victory in a crazy Game 5 that put Houston up three games to two heading back to Los Angeles.

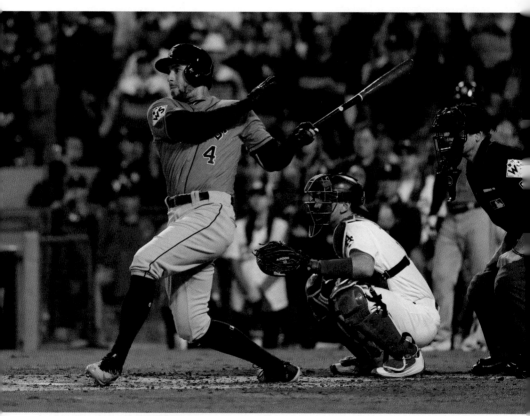

Springer, who hit .379 in the series, with five homers and seven RBIs, went 2-for-5 in Game 7, including this second-inning, two-run home run to put the Astros up 5–0. Springer was named the 2017 World Series MVP.

Lance McCullers Jr. (43), Brad Peacock (41), and Charlie Morton (below) collaborated (with $^2/_3$ innings from Francisco Liriano and Chris Devenski) to hold the Dodgers to just one run in Game 7. Over the course of the series, the three right-handers combined for a 2–0 record with a save, a 2.49 ERA, and 25 strikeouts in $25^1/_3$ innings pitched.

Catcher Brian McCann leaps into his pitcher's arms after Morton got Corey Seager to ground out to Altuve to end the game, 5–1 Astros, and give the series to Houston, four games to three.

The Houston Astros celebrate the franchise's first-ever World Series championship on the field at Dodger Stadium after defeating Los Angeles 5–1 in Game 7.

Keuchel was returning to his early season form, posting a 2.87 ERA in 31⅓ September innings. But what about McCullers, who had shown in 2015 and 2016 he could be one of the most dominant starting arms in the game when everything was right? With Verlander, Keuchel, Peacock, Charlie Morton, and Collin McHugh in the rotation, would the 23-year-old right-hander be a bigger asset for the Astros if he started firing out of the pen? "I've got to do what the team asks me," McCullers said. "I've got to help the team win. If they want to see me out of the pen, then that's their decision. Obviously, I want to start."

From August 1 to September 23, McCullers only took the mound once for the Astros. Against the Los Angeles Angels on September 24, he was sharp through two innings and left the mound with a two-run lead in his team's final regular-season home game of 2017. But McCullers only lasted for 3⅓ frames against the below-.500 Angels, and Los Angeles' Brandon Phillips golf-clubbed a shot onto Minute Maid Park's train tracks during McCullers' final abbreviated frame. When Hinch opened up his bullpen with five-plus innings to go on ESPN's *Sunday Night Baseball* broadcast, the postseason questions only continued about one of the Astros' most dangerous—but uncertain—arms and the overall state of the team's pitching staff. How much trust could the 95-win Astros place in McCullers when the real tests arrived?

"If he's healthy and in the strike zone, Lance is already ready to pitch in a postseason game," Hinch said. "He's really good. He has weapons to get anybody in the league out."

The last time the Astros had made the playoffs was still the high point of McCullers' young career. He debuted May 18, 2015, fired through four wins before June was complete, then entered October as a gutsy 21-year-old doubling as one of the sharpest arms on the staff. When the No. 41 overall pick of the 2012 amateur draft took the mound in Game 4 of the AL Division Series against Kansas City, the righty did his part for 6⅓ inspiring innings, allowing only two hits and two runs while striking out seven on 110 pitches (72 strikes). The Astros ultimately caved 9–6 to the eventual World Series champions in one of the cruelest playoff defeats in franchise history. But it was still 3–2 Astros when McCullers left the mound, and fans were left with the vision of a young fireballer with the heart and drive to match.

"I know what it feels like and I know what it takes to pitch there," McCullers said.

They were almost there.

From September 14 to October 1, the second-best regular-season team in Astros history won 14 of 17 games and finished its already-storybook 2017 season with a 4–3 victory against the Boston Red Sox at Fenway Park. The Rangers, an afterthought since May, were swept in Arlington, Texas. The Mariners, supposedly a division contender, also fell to Hinch's team in three straight games. And four final contests for the Astros in Boston ended up as three more victories for a 101-win team. Only the 1998 Astros had won more, and they had hit a wall by running into Kevin Brown's San Diego Padres, falling 3–1 in the National League Division Series.

Verlander was roaring. Keuchel was primed. Altuve had unleashed the best overall season of his career (MLB-best .346 average, 24 home runs, 81 RBIs, 112 runs, 32 stolen bases, .957 OPS) and was the smart choice for American League MVP as the playoffs approached. Correa and Springer were staring at their second shots at the postseason, while Bregman was waiting for his first.

The 2017 Astros had felt special since they first arrived in West Palm Beach, when everything was new, unboxed, and still under construction. They had been the best team in baseball in the spring, survived their summer test, finally added Verlander, endured Hurricanes Harvey and Maria, and were now heating up again at just the right time.

"The town's looking forward to it. Everywhere I go—every single restaurant I go to—the people are hyped," Correa said. "They let you know how grateful they are for the season we've had so far. But we always say, 'We're not done yet. We've got to accomplish a lot more.'"

The Astros' 23-year-old shortstop, an All-Star two seasons after his MLB debut at 20, was entering the playoffs with extra meaning. The double blow of Hurricanes Harvey and Maria was still on Correa's mind. "It was a tough month," he said. "Both of the hurricanes, for me, affecting both of my towns. I feel like Puerto Rico is my home. But Houston is my home as well, and now my adopted home. So it was tough. We had to figure out ways to help—just to be able to use your stage to help other people and impact other people's lives. Throughout all this tragedy, make them feel a little bit better, a little bit happier, it just means everything to us."

The Astros were a release.

The Cleveland Indians had 102 wins. The Los Angeles Dodgers had 104. The New York Yankees, Washington Nationals, and defending-champion Chicago Cubs all had real shots at this year's trophy. So did the Astros. And with Houston standing strong and united behind them, a thrilling team that won its division by 21 games was just getting started.

"Part of our job is to provide something to be proud of—and I think we have," Hinch said. "We're not done yet, and we want to make this the most special year of all time in this organization. But it starts in a couple days and will carry it as long as we keep winning. And I think the emotions that have gone into this month for a lot of people in our community kind of push us to want to deliver."

12

I GOT TO WAKE UP

To be honest with you, I already forgot about my batting title. This is a new season for me. A five-game series. We're going to do everything we can do to beat the Red Sox, to play good baseball, and we know we have the team to do it.

—José Altuve

THEY LOOKED BACK with perfect clarity, two years later, and admitted the truth: the first time felt like a rush. New York and Yankee Stadium under huge national-television lights. Then halfway across the country to Kansas City, Missouri. Then, finally, back to Houston, where the once-horrible Astros hosted their first playoff game in 10 long years before an ear-splitting crowd that just kept getting louder and louder...before it suddenly became silent.

Almost two years to the day that their magical 2015 season fell apart in the eighth inning of Game 4 of the ALDS against the eventual world champion Kansas City Royals, the Astros were back at Minute Maid Park. Older, wiser, and more experienced. No longer second place to the Texas Rangers; now AL West division winners with 101 victories to their name. And, in a sign of the rapidly changing times in major league baseball, favored against the storied Boston Red Sox, with the first two games of the 2017 ALDS in a rebuilding city that was rapidly becoming obsessed with its highly loveable Astros.

The 2015 season was the start of it all. By the end, the Astros just wanted to see how far they could go before their magic ran out and reality returned. Two years later, downtown Houston buzzed the morning before Game 1 against Boston, and belief kept building. These Astros really had a shot at winning it all—and they knew it.

"I think I've grown so much—I think mentally, and the experience I've acquired playing every single day for the last two years and a half," said shortstop Carlos Correa, who had just turned 23 and was far past his eighth-inning error in Game 4 versus the Royals. "Having guys in the clubhouse like [Carlos] Beltran has helped me a lot, as well. I talk baseball with him most of the time. And just watching José [Altuve] play every single day and the way he goes about his business. The biggest thing I've learned from him is, you got two hits in your first two at-bats, you got to have three, four hits that day. You can't just be pleased with having two hits that day. So that drives me every single day, the way he goes. He has four hits and he's like, 'Carlos, I never had a five-hit game before, let me try to get the fifth hit.' He's always striving for more. And that's what I've learned from him that makes me better every single day."

On the morning of October 4, "ALDS 2017" flashed on Minute Maid Park's jumbotron. The Astros were wrapped in "October Ready" T-shirts, oversized "H Strong" stickers were featured on the roofs of the ballpark's dugouts, and the stadium's roof was opened to reveal shining downtown Houston.

The double blows of Hurricanes Harvey and Maria were still in the Astros' minds. "It's been a short month since all of that happened, and we haven't forgotten about the hurricane," manager A.J. Hinch said. "We understand the patch we wear on our jersey and the amount that the city has rallied around us."

As the Astros waited for Boston—Hinch's team as loose, energetic, and carefree as ever—Beltran embraced owner Jim Crane behind the batting cage at Minute Maid Park. Many of Beltran's family members—including his 69-year-old mother, 70-year-old father, and brother—were in Houston thanks to Crane, who had provided a plane to help transport Puerto Rico residents affected by Maria. Other Astros players also used the plane to transport family off the island, while some cancer patients were aided so they could continue chemotherapy treatments.

"When Jim sent the plane to Puerto Rico, he sent like a 100-passenger plane, and he said, 'Carlos, if you need to get people out of Puerto Rico, let me know,'" said Beltran, after the Astros' final workout before Game 1. "First of all, I told my parents about it. They said, 'No.' And the last day they said, 'Okay, we're leaving.' We had a meeting here, and it was like a two-minute meeting. [Crane] said, 'Carlos, don't worry. We got it.'…And when you see that, for me, I can't thank him enough."

The ability to watch the Astros during Games 1 and 2 of the ALDS in Houston provided a much-needed break from the recovery after Maria. "My mom said that the day she got here, she took a shower and she said, 'Carlos, I took a shower and I spent like an hour in the shower. I've been showering with literally no water over there,'" Beltran said. "To hear that from my mom, it really broke my heart, because you don't want your parents to go through tough times."

Chris Sale and the 93-win, AL East champion Red Sox were also waiting. The further the Astros went into October, the more Houston would rally behind them. And if they reached the international platform of the World Series, the 2017 Astros could take their public joy to the next level and beyond. Houston knew just how special the Astros were. But the outside baseball world was mostly focusing on the Los Angeles Dodgers, Chicago Cubs, Cleveland Indians, Yankees, and Red Sox in early October, and still did not view the Astros as a true World Series favorite.

"One thing I know about this team is they're going to have fun and they're going to be themselves. They're not spooked by the moment," Hinch said. "The enjoyment that these guys had during the race—even the low moments this year…it's kind of funny to even talk about low moments in the kind of season we had—this team remained fun and good and upbeat and positive."

Hinch's club was set up perfectly heading into Game 1. Facing Sale, a power lefthander who went 17–8 with a 2.90 ERA and 308 strikeouts in 214⅓ innings during the regular season, was far from ideal. If the Astros dropped their first game in their own ballpark, the series would immediately turn. But 2011 AL Cy Young Award winner Justin Verlander was followed by 2015 AL Cy Young Award winner Dallas Keuchel, while the best hitting team in MLB—the Astros led the sport in runs scored (896), batting average (.282), and OPS (.823), and finished second in home runs (238)—was set up to constantly attack a top-heavy Boston rotation and a shaky Red Sox bullpen.

"This is a very complete team," Boston manager John Farrell said. "They're explosive offensively. They play well here at home. But we need to go out and focus on the control of things on our own end."

Hinch's first Astros team had made it through six playoff games before burning out in Game 5 of the ALDS. The 2017 Astros had the veterans the 2015 team lacked, confidence that had been building since February, and the unified belief that this playoff run was already about more than just baseball. "I expect it to be loud," Hinch said. "This is one of the loudest buildings I've ever been in, in 2015, during the playoffs. So I don't expect to be disappointed because of the way our crowd gets into it....It will be an incredible environment for us."

It got to the point where "incredible" was no longer enough to describe Altuve. He was a 17-year-old from Venezuela adjusting to so much all at once. He was 5'6", 165 pounds, and never even supposed to make the major leagues. He was a little-known, singles-hitting second baseman on the 106-loss 2011 Astros. And then he was the most dangerous hitter in the deepest lineup in MLB at 27, crushing three no-doubt home runs to rip open the start of an October playoff run that would last until November 1.

By the end of Game 1, Altuve could not walk to the plate at sold-out Minute Maid Park without 43,102 fans proudly shouting,

"MVP! MVP! MVP!!!" in his face. His third shot was blasted over the Crawford Boxes, rocketing toward glass, sunlight, and downtown Houston. At that point—surreal, earsplitting, perfectly ridiculous—Altuve told himself to snap out of it and just wake up. It could not be real. He literally had to be dreaming.

"I couldn't believe any of my homers," said Altuve, who went 3-for-4 in the Astros' 8–2 beatdown of the Red Sox in Game 1. "I hit one and I was like, 'Wow.' And the second one is like, 'Wow, what's going on here?' And it feels great. If I can do—everything I can do to help my team in this kind of game, I'm going to feel happy to do it. Because one thing I can tell you is we have a lot of talent out there and…the energy we brought today is the energy we need to play the rest of the games."

Babe Ruth. Reggie Jackson. George Brett. Albert Pujols. Altuve. The face of the Astros became just the ninth player in MLB history to hit three home runs in a postseason game and the first Astro since the franchise began in 1962.

"First off, how good is José Altuve?" said Hinch, opening his post-win press conference by again praising No. 27. "I mean, that is such a good day for him personally, for our team. No surprise to those of us who have been with the Astros or following the Astros for a long time. It's incredible to watch him step up and be every bit the star that we needed today, for sure. It's hard to describe in different ways. The local media here is probably bored with how I talk about him, but he's exceptional and he's prepared. And he went out today and kept a really calm heartbeat and got pitches to hit and did incredible damage."

Each new blast created hope that the Astros really could do it all: ALDS, ALCS, World Series.

Alex Bregman inspired Altuve with a first-inning solo shot. Do-everything Marwin González delivered with a perfectly timed two-run double in the fourth. And the Astros knocked Sale out of the game with nine hits and seven runs in five battered innings.

Then Altuve—who never hit more than seven homers during his initial four seasons—went deep in the first, fifth, and seventh for a combined 1,206 feet of inspirational power.

"José, he's an incredible baseball player," said Verlander, who just kept winning as an Astro, recording a six-inning, two-run victory during his playoff debut for Houston. "Against one of the toughest pitchers in all of baseball, he just finds a way to barrel baseballs....I had the pleasure of playing with Miguel Cabrera [in Detroit] for a long time, and it never failed how great he was. People, when we got new teammates, after a couple weeks, it never failed somebody would be like, 'Wow, playing against him I knew how great he was, but playing with him, he's even better.' And that's like the ultimate compliment, and that's the compliment I can give to Altuve, because since I've been here, man, it's been a lot of fun to watch, and he's a very special ballplayer."

Altuve was stunned in the aftermath. He thanked God for an "incredible game." He recalled looking up at the scoreboard after it was 8–2 Astros and thinking, "Wow...we did it." After the third no-doubter? "I got to wake up," Altuve told himself. He also drew raves from Hall of Famer Craig Biggio, who had become the Astros' official link between the franchise's past and present.

"He's a great player and he hit three different pitches," Biggio said. "It's just exciting and fun to watch. It's been fun to watch him evolve, from the player when he first got here to who he is now. And we're excited to have him with our uniform on."

It was the Astros' first playoff game after Hurricane Harvey. And the 2017 AL MVP hit three home runs in one day in downtown Houston, as the Astros destroyed the Red Sox: eight runs, 12 hits, and game over by the sixth inning, while Minute Maid Park just kept getting louder.

"I think we can officially call him a 'run producer,'" Hinch said. "In a lot of ways, he gets so many hits that I think some of his run production gets cast aside a little bit. But he's the best hitter in the league, and that's in a league of really, really good hitters. And to watch him have a day like today, it's a great reward for the work that's put in to not only be a good hitter who gets hits, but be a good hitter who produces runs, and that's not easy to do at this level."

In Game 2, the names would be different—George Springer, Evan Gattis, Chris Devenski, Keuchel, Correa—but it did not matter. This was the way the Astros had done it all season. Someone new would come through when he had to. Altuve was the best hitter in baseball and would win the MVP in the year of Aaron Judge. But the Astros did not solely rely on him and would put up eight runs again the next day. Verlander had been unbeatable since he relocated his life to Houston. The next game, the Astros' No. 2 arm would match the new ace, and the team that had blown a 2–1 series lead in the 2015 ALDS now had three games to close out the fading Red Sox.

"You've seen it throughout the whole season," said Correa, who went 2-for-4 with a two-run home run in the first inning off Boston lefthander Drew Pomeranz and ended up with a game-high four RBIs in another 8–2 victory in Game 2. "There's a difference here of every single game, one through nine, everybody can do damage, everybody can go deep. That's the good thing about our lineup—there's no holes in our lineup, and we feel very confident, no matter if we went 0-for-4 the day before or if we went 4-for-4."

Altuve just continued to rip. He was 2-for-3 with an RBI, two runs, and two walks in his three-home-run follow-up, while the Astros' bats knocked Pomeranz out in the third inning before he could record a single out. Three relievers backed Keuchel (one run, seven strikeouts in $5^{2}/_{3}$ innings) with $3^{1}/_{3}$ innings of one-run ball, and the Astros again ended up with 12 hits in the second consecutive beatdown of Boston.

More than 86,000 fans had watched the Astros take Games 1 and 2 against one of MLB's most-storied teams. With Fenway Park and a trip to the Northeast looming, Minute Maid Park roared like it knew the ALCS would soon replace the ALDS in Houston. And the lineup that general manager Jeff Luhnow constructed during the off-season was peaking at the right time.

"We're judged over 162 to get to this point, and we put up some pretty good numbers," Hinch said. "We have a number of guys who have contributed. So, obviously, you're seeing what's possible when we link things together and the hitters start to feed off of one another. We have a lot of guys who are putting up really good at-bats. So where it fits in the whole spectrum is up to you guys, but we're pretty confident that when we put good at-bats together, we're going to score runs from a couple different spots of the order. Altuve still had a pretty good day—four times on base. But other guys in our lineup are here to hit, too. It's nice to have that many threats throughout the order any given day."

The Astros' young Core Four was doing the most damage: Springer, Bregman, Altuve, and Correa. A united group of young names and instantly familiar faces who had battered the Red Sox for a combined .375 average, six home runs, and 10 RBIs during Games 1 and 2 of the ALDS. When the foursome showed up in a legendary ballpark during a series off-day, up 2–0 and with two road games to suddenly end Boston's season, they strode onto a famous field with all the confidence that youth, talent, and a grow-ing sense of inevitability bring. This was their time, and they were perfectly comfortable on top of the baseball world. They were also Hinch's 1–4 hitters, and if you managed to pitch around one, the next young bat was going to make you pay.

"We feel like we're brothers and we've got to take care of each other, on and off the field," Correa said.

The national spotlight was beginning to zoom in tighter on the 2017 Astros, and Fenway Park was the perfect elevated stage. As talking heads praised the Astros' young talent and opined about just how special the rebuilt team could be into the next decade, the conversation always came back to the impossible-to-ignore potential of the Core Four. The Astros filled up three-fourths of their infield with the foursome, all were under team-friendly contracts, and none had to worry about turning 30 any time soon.

"The most impressive thing for me about the group is how much value they add on all facets of the game," general manager Jeff Luhnow said. "These are four extremely athletic baseball players. Each of them could play probably any position on the field if they chose to dedicate themselves to it. The combination of the defense, the base running, the power, the batting eye, the contact ability—I mean, this is a really special group of four players, and they get along really well with each other. You don't get that everywhere. You've got two Americans, one Puerto Rican, and one Venezuelan, but you would never know that they didn't grow up together, didn't go to high school together. It's pretty cool."

That's also what made the Core Four so special: they liked each other. October 7 at Fenway began with Altuve, Springer, and Correa cracking each other up next to the batting cage—even the 34-year-old Verlander could not help but laugh at the inside jokes. Soon Altuve, Correa, and Bregman were united near second base—33-year-old Yuli Gurriel was allowed to join the party—in another laughfest. When a ball was ripped into center field, Correa yanked his teammates down all at once. Seconds later, the heroic move was followed with more laughter.

"It's just unbelievable to see the chemistry," Correa said. "We were just talking about it during [batting practice], how much we love this team. Because everybody gets along, everybody has talent on this team, and any given night anybody can be the hero."

Bregman was just as upbeat on an off-day. "We have so much fun playing every single day," he said. "We want to do that forever. We think that we can have a great team for a lot of years to come, and we want to play together for a long time."

Now that the Astros finally had players their fans knew, followed, and loved—there were no thunderous home-crowd MVP chants during the rebuilding years—they were already making plans to keep their young stars in uniform for as long as possible. "We certainly don't plan to move any of them any time soon," Luhnow said. "So it's just a matter of whether or not when their contracts are up and they become free agents, whether or not we can convince them to stick around. I certainly would like to have all four of those guys here for certainly as long as I'm here."

A day away from starting Game 3, Brad Peacock referred to the core of the Astros' resurgence as "awesome." "I played with Springer and Bregman in the minor leagues and just watching Correa come up, I knew they were going to be something special, and they were just unbelievable—fun to watch, bring high energy," said Peacock, who was about 24 hours away from tossing his final bullpen warmup ball to his father. "It's what you need. You need a bunch of...young guys who keep everybody up on their toes, and they're just fun to watch every day."

Game 3 began nearly the same as the previous two. In the first inning, Springer led off with a single, took second on a Doug Fister wild pitch, and scored when Josh Reddick sent a 91-mph fastball into center field. An Altuve ground-out pushed Reddick to third. Then Correa blasted a 385-foot home run to deep center, trading a 74-mph curve for a 3–0 Astros lead after one.

By the top of the second inning, the ALDS was a few feet away from being over. After putting up 16 runs in Games 1 and 2, the Astros almost made it 6–0 in Game 3 when Reddick lifted a slider to the right-field corner with runners on second and third. Correa later described the near-home run as a "knockout" blow. But Boston's Mookie Betts stretched out, Reddick's shot ended up in a glove instead of the stands, and the Red Sox finally woke up by answering with four runs in their next two frames.

"That was a huge momentum shift that we later felt," Hinch said. "I don't know that we necessarily felt it right there. We felt we were in a good spot. It was 3–0 at the time. Going to 6–0 there would have really put them in a hole. So obviously as the ball was carrying, it's probably out of most ballparks. If he hooks it a little bit more, it's gone.…There's such small margins in these games and huge moments throughout the entire day."

The remainder of Game 3 was devoted to second guessing and the Red Sox's revival. Peacock was only given 2²/₃ innings, despite constantly bailing out the Astros throughout the regular season. By the time a 10–3 Boston win was official, Hinch had been forced to use five relievers, and Fenway Park had come alive in a brutal six-run seventh—three Astros relievers were required just to get three outs. The joyous sway of "Sweet Caroline" was followed with a defiant "I Won't Back Down." Boston's heartbeat was back.

"We're going to be fine. We'll bounce back out of this and come back and play hard," said Hinch, after his club watched its series lead shrink to 2–1. "But this is playoff baseball. If anybody thought the Red Sox were going to lay down, probably rethink it."

Focus and resilience carried the Astros through 162 regular-season contests and Games 1 and 2 of the ALDS. They began 2017 as the hottest club in baseball, leapt out to the fastest start in franchise history, then fought off major injuries to the rotation and lineup to still win 101 games and finish with the third-best record in MLB.

Inside a cramped visitor's clubhouse, with TV cameras and microphones hovering near his face, a key member of the Astros' Core Four sounded like a team spokesman. "I'm confident we're going to go out there [Monday] like nothing happened [Sunday] and hopefully go back home with a victory," Correa said.

Then the 23-year-old shortstop acknowledged the significance of Game 4. Even with a loss, the Astros would still have the series finale back home at Minute Maid Park. But the Red Sox had a history of unbelievable revivals, while the Astros' 2015 season had been silenced by Game 4 heartbreak in the ALDS against the Royals. This was a calm, cool team that rarely lost its swagger. But even Correa knew that closing out the Red Sox in Boston was an opportunity these Astros could not afford to miss.

"It's very significant. It's really important....We don't want to go back home and have a Game 5," he said. "But at the same time, there's no need to put pressure on ourselves. We've been working through 162 games and playing solid baseball. Now is the time we've got to show it."

October 9 began and ended with rain. Fall was settling in, and the streets around Fenway Park were colored with umbrellas, raincoats, and red-and-blue ponchos. In the morning hours, there was serious doubt as to whether Game 4 would even be played, while the Sunday evening announcement of Monday's start time had been held up due to the New York Yankees' all-powerful TV presence.

"The number one question for us is, how long was the rain going to stay off or when was it going to come or what was going to happen," Hinch said. "So we thought it could be a broken game from the very beginning."

The rain eased up just in time for the first pitch. Veteran right-hander Charlie Morton faced righty Rick Porcello, who had won the 2016 AL Cy Young Award. And for the next four hours and seven minutes, the Astros and Red Sox played one of the best playoff games in Fenway Park history.

It was 1–0 Astros in the top of the first. Then it was 1–1 heading into the second. It was 2–1 Astros in the top of the second, then it was 3–2 Boston in the bottom of the fifth as the rain returned and a slow-arriving crowd did everything within its power to keep the Red Sox's season alive.

Farrell was ejected, in what became his final game managing Boston. Springer and Gurriel collected three hits apiece for the Astros; the Red Sox's 2–7 hitters combined for nine. And by the time the skies had darkened and the day-long predicted rain finally began to pour down, Hinch had turned Verlander into a reliever for the first time in his 13-year career, while Boston had gotten 4²/₃ innings of four-hit, two-run ball out of Sale, who took the mound in the top of the fourth and nearly pushed the Red Sox to Game 5 back in Houston.

In all three playoff series, there were moments when it felt like the Astros' season was slipping away. After Betts robbed Reddick in Game 3, Fenway Park was soon taunting him, and the Red Sox's 10–3 blowout gave Boston new life. After Hinch had missed on his decision to use unpredictable reliever Francisco Liriano in Game 3, the Astros' manager was initially second-guessed even harder when he gave the ball to Verlander in Game 4.

"We talked to Verlander before the game and just said, 'Hey, if Charlie goes and then there's a pause or there's a break in the action and we need to resume and we have the lead, we may turn to you for the bridge to try to get to [Ken] Giles,'" Hinch said. "And the game didn't end up that way, right? It ended up the rain came on and off again....And then as the game unfolded and we got the lead, I felt really good about it. And Justin Verlander wanted the ball."

Months later, the decision to bring Verlander out of the pen would be celebrated as a confident, gutsy move that set up the Astros' unorthodox reliever pattern in the World Series. But on a rainy Monday afternoon at Fenway, Verlander's fifth pitch to Andrew Benintendi became a two-run blast that ended up in the right-field seats to give Boston a 3–2 lead. At the time, it only felt like the beginning of another collapse.

"I was deflated. There's no question," Luhnow said. "Demoralized. All the words you can use that our fans were feeling. I knew it was early enough in the game and we've done so well in the late innings. And I knew that at some point [Chris] Sale was going to start to get tired and we would get into some of the rest of their bullpen. But at that point, I started to think about, *Okay, Game 5, what are we looking at here?* You like a Game 5 in Houston with

Keuchel on the mound. But at the same time, you prefer skipping it altogether."

The Astros had blown Game 3 after nearly going up 6–0 and were now suddenly down in Game 4. Boston had Sale rolling on the mound, and Fenway was believing in the Red Sox again. "Losing Game 3, we got our butts kicked. It just kind of felt like 2015 all over again," Keuchel said. "As soon as we gave up the lead in the fifth, it seemed like the air was shot out of us."

As Verlander tried to find a foothold against Sale, Keuchel turned to his teammates and said enough. It was a veteran motivational move that Verlander would later replicate during Game 2 of the World Series. This was not 2015 and just another playoff collapse for the Astros and the city of Houston. This was 2017. These Astros were making a stand and shutting down Boston's season.

"I was reminding them, 'Hey, we are the best team. We are the best team in the American League,'" Keuchel said. "When you look at it, we have the best lineup in the American League. There's no doubt about it. It's amazing that even the best lineup, the best team, can get deflated at some point."

The best-hitting team in baseball gritted it out again. A Bregman solo blast off Sale over the Green Monster tied the game at 3–3. A 3–2 deficit and just six outs to go had somehow become a tie ballgame and a stunned Fenway. Who was this team that just would not go away? Then, after a Gattis single, Craig Kimbrel came in to relieve a suddenly shaky Sale. He promptly threw a wild pitch and walked Springer to keep the eighth going. Reddick took three balls and fouled off four pitches before perfectly placing a 99-mph Kimbrel fastball past the shortstop and into left field for a 4–3 lead. Springer sprinted across the dirt, grasped onto third base, and proudly pointed across the diamond at his teammate who had silenced Fenway.

"I haven't been a part of anything like [this] in my career, and I've been a part of some pretty special teams," said Reddick afterward, again wearing his celebratory American flag Speedo. "This is a team that can do a lot of special things."

Beltran then doubled to deep left field in the ninth, giving the Astros an extra run that would prove crucial in a messy, tight, and nerve-wracking Game 4 on October 9 that ultimately ended 5–4 Houston and gave the Astros a 3–1 series victory over the Red Sox in the ALDS.

"I had all the confidence in the world that we were going to find a way to scratch and claw like we have done all year and get the lead back," Bregman said. "I was in the dugout, and [bench coach] Alex Cora came up to me and said, 'Hey, one at-bat, that's all that matters.'...I was fortunate enough to get a good pitch to hit and put a good swing on it."

They came back out one more time, just to make sure it was real. Fenway Park emptied out in October. The Red Sox finished and done. Huge stadium lights shining over a famous field and the hard rain finally falling. Then it was Hinch's Astros screaming in unison before gathering near the mound for a team picture that would last forever.

"We envisioned ourselves being here since the beginning of the year, and nothing really changes on our end," Bregman said. "We're going to keep showing up to the yard every day, having fun, competing, playing the game the right way, playing it hard, and playing for each other. I think honestly this game, going to Game 4, coming down to the wire in a hostile environment's going to help us for the rest of the postseason and give us confidence moving forward."

The Astros were four wins from the World Series and eight from a world championship. They also never had to feel the pain of their collapse in 2015 ever again.

Altuve, Correa, Springer, González, Keuchel, and Lance McCullers Jr. had been forced to live with and hear about Game 4 against Kansas City for two long years. Six outs, six outs, six outs. Those crushed Astros never forgot. And they always knew the only way to truly move forward was to not let their next ALDS slip away.

"These players on this team that were here in 2015 have never stopped talking about it or have forgotten about that moment," said McCullers, as beer and champagne sprayed around him and the Astros rampaged inside Fenway's cramped visitors' clubhouse. "We wanted to redeem ourselves. There are a lot of the same guys here that experienced that day. And I tell you, it was the most gut-wrenching, depressing month I've ever had happen in my life. I couldn't watch baseball. I didn't want to talk about baseball or the World Series or anything....The fans who were there who have stuck with us and have ridden this wave out with us, they deserve to celebrate like we do."

The Red Sox were done.

It was time for the New York Yankees.

13

BRING YOUR EARPLUGS

When I see orange-out or white-out and all those towels—I look over at Keuchel's Korner and see a bunch of fake beards—it really gives you a sense of calmness almost in such a chaotic atmosphere. So that alone makes me feel like I'm in my backyard playing Wiffle ball, and right now just the thought of it is giving me chills. But to be hosting the Championship Series is going to be truly special. To have four games in a seven-game series is going to be very valuable....To have the crowds back, to have the fans back, to have the city behind us, it really gives us that extra boost.

—Astros pitcher Dallas Keuchel

IT TOOK UNTIL October 13 for the 101-win Astros to receive a proper national stage.

Major league baseball loves its legacy teams. But even an American League Division Series against the storied Boston Red Sox could not get the Astros onto national prime-time television. It took the arrival of the even-more-storied New York Yankees in the American League Championship Series for the Astros to actually receive an evening slot on TV.

The defending World Series–champion Chicago Cubs needed all five games to take down the Washington Nationals in the NLDS. The 104-win Los Angeles Dodgers blanked the Arizona Diamondbacks 3–0 in their NLDS matchup, then waited for the Cubs for an NLCS ready-made for TV. But after downing the Red Sox in the Fenway Park rain on October 9, the Astros had to wait for a winner between the 102-win Cleveland Indians and the Yankees. And it took New York's come-from-behind triumph—Joe Girardi's resilient wild-card team turned a 2–0 hole against the AL's best regular-season team into a stunning 3–2 ALDS victory over Cleveland—just to bring an official national baseball spotlight to Houston.

"I didn't expect when we were playing the Division Series... [against] the Red Sox, that we would be playing so many day games just because of how storied their tradition is as well," said Astros lefthander Dallas Keuchel, who was set to take the ball in Game 1 of the ALCS against New York right-hander Masahrio Tanaka. "I know the media markets in New York and L.A. are just so much more powerful, just because it's the East and West Coast. But at this point, we won 101 games—we don't need to prove anything. [Carlos] Correa has done very well against the Yankees. [José] Altuve is the MVP, so everybody knows his name, and [Alex] Bregman's going to be the same way. But we're so much more than just that. I know a lot of guys do like the flash and like the prime-time games, and that's good for them—whatever gets you up for these types of games, then let it get you up for it. But when it comes down to it, we'll be playing baseball. But it is a little bit more fun to be playing such...back-to-back storied franchises, with the Red Sox and the Yankees."

Four years after losing 111 games, A.J. Hinch's Astros were four wins away from the World Series. And what a perfect path Houston's baseball team had been presented as it approached the 2017 Fall Classic. Battering Boston for two raucous ALDS blowouts at Minute Maid Park, then fighting off the Red Sox at Fenway Park for a 3–1 series victory and a rain-covered celebration. After waiting to learn who their ALCS opponent would be, it was then the legendary Yankees walking across the outfield in downtown Houston, with Hinch's Astros holding home-field advantage and New York as the wild-card underdog.

The Astros' time had finally arrived. Overcome the Red Sox and Yankees—232 seasons, 76 playoff appearances, and 35 championships combined—on the way to the World Series, and the buzz surrounding the 2017 Astros would start to scream.

"I expect it to be loud and I expect it to be pretty pro-Astros....I love the fact that we're opening up at home," Hinch said. "Other than the Indians, in the American League nobody had more wins. So it took a lot to get us to have this right. But to sleep in our own beds a couple times, to play in front of our home fans, we hope to get off to a hot start in a seven-game series. Sign me up for four home games and three road games if it takes seven games. The environment's going to be crazy. The people here are hungry for baseball. They have been passionate about this team. This is an easy team to fall in love with—it's been that way since the beginning of the season. Roof closed can be pretty hot...and get pretty loud. So bring your earplugs, be ready. It's a pretty loud environment."

Keuchel had first announced the Astros' arrival in 2015, when Hinch's team had traveled to Yankee Stadium on little rest, then silenced New York 3–0 in a wild-card game. But two years later, the baseball world was mesmerized with just how big and tall the 6'7", 282-pound Aaron Judge was when he stood next to the 5'6", 165-pound José Altuve. Ringing national praise? The accepted understanding that Houston was a baseball city again and these Astros were just as deep and dangerous as anyone else left in the 2017 playoffs? That was still to come.

"This organization has come a long way. We're very proud of that," Hinch said. "It's a very proud organization that a lot of people before me have helped pave the way to get this franchise to where we're at. And we have a tremendous opportunity with a good team. I think our guys embrace that. We play in a great city, a great fan base. There's a lot of positive mojo going on around here with this team."

Before Game 1, the Yankees—who had won Game 5 of the ALDS on the road against the 102-win Indians—were widely viewed as ahead of schedule and peaking at the right time. But New York also held the second-highest payroll in MLB, had nine veterans 30 or older, had signed closer Aroldis Chapman to a record-setting $86 million contract, and were more win-now than the Astros at the initial July 31 trade deadline.

Jeff Luhnow's rebuilt Astros were also ahead of schedule. Four wins from the franchise's second World Series appearance, the sixth-year general manager had never looked so right. The Astros had invested in themselves and built an annual contender. But they had also evolved and adapted over time, and were now approaching a platform that had been teased when the rebuild began.

"We earned it. We played day games because we're not the prime-time show," Luhnow said. "But that allowed us to be the first team to clinch, and I think there's an advantage there....This is going to be a really exciting championship series."

Every significant accomplishment since the franchise's reconstruction began had felt like a milestone for the team. Hosting the ALCS against the Yankees was the Astros' highest peak to date. "Winning the wild-card game in 2015 in New York, that felt so huge to us," Luhnow said. "But you look at what other clubs have done and some clubs struggled to get out of the first round, even with very good teams. Having been to the Division Series and lost in five games [in 2015], we wanted it so badly. And in Game 4 [against Boston] when we got behind, you sort of felt like, 'Oh, no. Could this be slipping away from us?' And there was a sense of accomplishment after that—almost a sigh of relief that, 'Okay, we got past this first round. This team is now in the final four.'... Once you're in the final four, you know that every team you face is going to be excellent. But you also know that you have a pretty good chance to win two more series and win the championship."

Then the GM, who had added Josh Reddick and ex-Yankees Brian McCann and Carlos Beltran during a critical off-season, sounded prophetic: "Our strengths play well in a seven-game series, because of the depth of our offense," he said before the ALCS began. "We're going to have a game or two where our offense is going to go cold, especially considering the pitching we're about to face. But to keep these guys down for more than a game, I think is going to be really tough for the opposition. Our pitching matches up with just about anybody we're going to face, and our offense, in my opinion, is better. I like our chances."

Then Keuchel and Justin Verlander took the mound before a constantly roaring crowd. The Astros looked like a World Series team from the first inning of the ALCS. Fiery. Relentless. Precise. Marwin González, Altuve, Keuchel, and nine sharp innings of Astros baseball before 43,116 at Minute Maid Park. Hinch's club carved out a two-run lead against the hottest team in the playoffs, then held on for a tight 2–1 victory over the Yankees in Game 1.

"It was definitely more electric tonight than I had anticipated, and none of us, besides [Carlos] Beltran and I think a couple other guys, had been past the Division Series," said Keuchel, who struck out 10 on 109 pitches, while only allowing four New York hits in seven shutout innings. "We knew what the Division Series was going to be like, but it was just a whole other atmosphere tonight. That's what happens when you have the last two American League teams standing and fighting it out. So we can't say enough about our fans, the way they rallied around us and the way we have rallied around them....It's almost like a family setting. I can 100 percent say that I was getting a little tired there at the end and, honestly, they were pushing me through it, just the way the crowd was getting into it. And you don't see a lot of knowledgeable crowds when you go place to place, and this place is definitely one of the most knowledgeable places. In the game they know exactly what's going on and when to get up and when to boo and this and that."

Keuchel personally rolled the clock back to 2015, when he owned Minute Maid Park all season, then shredded New York at Yankee Stadium during the Astros' first postseason win in a decade. He was Cy Young–like again in Game 1 of the 2017 ALCS, firing away among piercing woos and clapping "Let's Go, Astros!" chants. The lefty became the first pitcher in playoff history to record two consecutive scoreless starts against the Yankees with at least seven innings and seven strikeouts.

"He was so good tonight and locked in mentally, he didn't give in at all," Hinch said. "He was very convicted in his game plan. He controlled the bottom part of the strike zone—he even climbed a couple times—he had a good cutter, he had a swing-and-miss breaking ball, made huge pitches to end some innings. Got a little bit of defensive help on some big plays and just continued to go out and got stronger as the game went on, which is an impressive characteristic when a starting pitcher can finish an outing the way that he did at a relative high pitch count at this time of year. You don't see a ton of guys get into the low 100 [pitches]. So very, very excellent performance."

As the Astros' bearded one silenced New York yet again—62 Ks and just seven earned runs in 57²/₃ career innings versus the Yankees—a stadium packed everywhere the eye could see knew what it was staring at. A 101-win team three victories away from the World Series. The second-best club in franchise history doing exactly what it had done since April: finding another way to claim another game, blending All-Stars with the severely underrated.

At the plate, Altuve went 3-for-4, while MVP rival Aaron Judge was 1-for-3, but struck out for the 17th time in 27 playoff at-bats. Closer Ken Giles then erased five Yankees as the third hour of Game 1 unfolded, racking up his second consecutive extended shutdown. Of course, Altuve—hitting .579 (11-for-19) in the playoffs—did it all and started his feisty club off with his standard brilliant spark.

"He's a great player. He's one of the best players in all of base-ball and we know that," Girardi said. "You have to make your pitches, and he's going to fight you tooth and nail. And his hand-eye coordination is off the charts. I mean, it's really off the charts. He doesn't swing and miss a lot. You would think with a guy that's aggressive, sometimes there's going to be swing and miss, but he's not. So he's got an unbelievable gift, and he knows how to use it."

The 2017 batting champion raced down the first-base line to barely beat out a throw from Yankees second baseman Starlin Castro, creating an infield single that became the Astros' first hit off Tanaka and setting up the first breakthrough of the game. Altuve then put on his MVP cape, stealing second while Correa was at the plate. Next a 23-year-old who had thrived under the spotlight since his major league debut ripped a single to left field, sending Altuve home and giving the home team a 1–0 lead. Minute Maid Park beamed and burnt orange, reaching its loudest volume of an already-cranked playoffs. Yuli Gurriel—Altuve-like since Game 3 of the ALDS, 10-for-20 overall in the postseason to that point—lifted the roof higher, lining an RBI single to center field and handing Keuchel a 2–0 advantage.

"What started out as an incredibly tight pitchers' duel, we felt like we had a huge lead at 2–0. Even though we know it's very, very small," Hinch said. "So not a surprise that José is involved and doing instinctual things on the bases, and also not a surprise that Dallas responded by continuing to pitch well."

When Judge did not strike out but instead lifted a two-out liner to left field, it appeared the Yankees were also about to break through. Enter González. The do-everything super utility man—who could have been the Astros' seventh All-Star—collected Judge's liner, reared back, and fired as Greg Bird rounded third and aimed for a piece of home. McCann—former Yankee and critical to Keuchel's mound attack—tagged Bird just before his leg reached the plate. It was still 2–0 Astros and remained so until Giles gave up a two-out homer to Greg Bird in the ninth, before holding on to close out a 2–1 Astros win in Game 1.

"You can't really say enough about the play of Marwin the whole season," Keuchel said. "He's literally the most undervalued player in the big leagues. And now that we got national attention, we're seeing everybody's worth."

Another breaking point waited. But, at the time, Game 2 of the ALCS was the highest point of the Astros' season.

Even if Hinch had tried to remove the ball from his new ace's hands before the 124th pitch of Game 2, the manager knew exactly what Verlander would say. *Go away. This is still my game to win. I'm not leaving the mound.*

Verlander's baseball hero and childhood idol, Nolan Ryan, watched the old-school beauty behind home plate. And when Correa and Altuve gathered before the Astros' eruption in the ninth inning, they told themselves they had to finish off the Yankees in Verlander's honor. "I would have had to rip the ball away from that man if I was going to take him out," said Hinch, after Correa ripped a game-winning double to right field. Altuve kept racing toward home, and the Astros celebrated another tight 2–1 victory—handing them a 2–0 advantage in the ALCS—by going crazy at Minute Maid Park, in one of the most thrilling playoff finishes in franchise history.

"It's the greatest feeling ever," Correa said. "Winning is always fun, but winning in the playoffs and such an important spot is even bigger. So really glad he was able to score."

Verlander set it all up and was the real story of Game 2. He agreed to change his life at the last minute just before August became September, suddenly agreeing to become a Houstonian. Since then, the 34-year-old right-hander had arrived at Minute Maid Park on the day the Astros started playing home games again after Hurricane Harvey, dominated the mound on the day his new team captured the AL West, shut down Boston in Game 1 of the

AL Division Series, emerged out of the pen for the first time in his career to help clinch Game 4, then silenced New York 2–1 in Game 2 of the ALCS. By October 14, Verlander was a stunning 8–0 with 59 strikeouts and just eight earned runs in 51⅔ innings as an Astro. It was not a coincidence that his new team was just two wins away from the World Series.

"This is what I envisioned when I made that decision. When it came down to it, when I decided to say yes, these are the moments that you envision," said Verlander, who set a career playoff high with 13 strikeouts and limited the Yankees to five hits and one earned run in nine winning innings. "You don't envision going 5–0 in the regular season once you get here. That's all fine and great, but that's not why I was brought here. I was brought here to help this team win a championship. And I'm aware of that, and I'm going to do everything I possibly can....I'm pretty tired right now, honestly, it's pretty mentally exhausting, the playoffs. But that's what it's all about, man, this is. After that game is over and just kind of sitting in the clubhouse and having my teammates come over and say how much they appreciated that effort, that's what it's all about. That means everything to me."

During an era when starters are praised for just going seven innings, Verlander went the full, strong nine. There were ringing shouts and constant cheers in the eighth. Then the instant recognition of the rare and special during the final frame, with Minute Maid Park standing as one and proudly claiming Verlander as its own.

"That was probably the loudest I heard a ballpark, or close to it," Verlander said. "And I've been part of some pretty loud moments. The way those fans were pushing me to finish that game—or finish the ninth inning and have a chance to win the game—I mean that matters. It gets your adrenaline going."

Before Chapman, the Yankees' fireballer, took over and extra innings could become a reality, Correa turned to his close friend and spoke the truth. We've got to do this for the team, Correa told Altuve. We've got to come through right now.

"He's like, 'Okay, let's do it,'" Correa said. "So he got a base hit, and I said, 'Okay, I got to do something here.'…So 3–2 count, I was just trying to get on top of a fastball, and [Chapman] threw a good fastball to hit, and I hit it in the gap."

Third-base coach Gary Pettis windmilled Altuve toward home. Judge's throw arrived early, then bounced around near home plate. The Astros leapt and shouted, making all 124 of Verlander's pitches count. The aggressive base running that began during Hinch's first year with the Astros in 2015 paid off in Game 2 of the ALCS— Altuve and Correa had literally manufactured a game-winning run.

"They were aggressive, we had a shot at home, the ball short-hopped [catcher Gary Sanchez], and he wasn't able to come up with it," Girardi said. "If he comes up with it, it's an out. He wasn't able to come up with it."

On August 31, the Astros added Verlander at the last minute, just for moments like this. In Game 2 of the ALCS, Verlander won it for the Astros. "Big moments are meant for big-time performers," Hinch said. "From pitch one, Justin Verlander was big for this team. Really, pitch one as an Astro. But most importantly, this game today he was exceptional in every way. From controlling his emotions to executing every pitch to being dominant with his fastball, the put-away breaking ball, a couple change-ups. He just was every bit the top-end pitcher in the league that he's been for a really long time. This is such a big moment for our team. But he put us on his back today with his pitching."

The Astros were so confident and strong in Houston. Then they cracked in New York.

There was only one drawback to the Astros' 2–0 ALCS lead: Hinch's club had scored just four runs total in the two games. The light hitting was transported to Yankee Stadium. When the Astros left New York, they were in a 3–2 series hole, and their storybook 2017 season was one defeat away from officially being over.

"The message to this team is going to be keep fighting the fight," Hinch said. "This series isn't over. This game is. We're going to get back to Houston and get an off-day with our families and come back ready to play."

Game 3 belonged to veteran lefthander CC Sabathia, who threw six shutout innings and struck out five on 99 pitches (64 strikes). It was 8–0 Yankees after four frames, and the Astros did not score until the ninth, marking the second time in their last five games that they had been blown out by an AL East opponent.

"I'm not surprised what [Sabathia] did tonight," Girardi said. "We talked about it—we wanted him on the mound tonight. We thought we had the right guy on the mound tonight. Again, six innings, just an outstanding effort. Couldn't ask for anything more."

The Yankees scored eight runs on seven hits—three-run home runs by Todd Frazier and Judge changed the game—while the Astros only managed four hits and their top-of-the-lineup Core Four was just 3-for-16 with five strikeouts. The Astros still held the series advantage. But a messy Game 3 had revived New York—mirroring Boston's resurgence in the AL Division Series—and the Yankees still had two more home games to make a stand.

"CC was really good because he didn't make a lot of mistakes," Hinch said. "We swung a little bit to the margins on the outside of the strike zone a little bit. But he can pitch with the elevated fastball. He's got a pretty good breaking ball, especially when he gets you in the swing mode. We were a little swing happy tonight against him, and he took advantage of being able to pitch to the outer parts of the strike zone."

In September, Lance McCullers Jr.'s status was one of the Astros' biggest question marks as the playoffs approached. Starter? Late-inning reliever? Bridge arm? Just as importantly: what could the

Astros realistically expect from one of their strongest but also most unpredictable arms? After Game 3 went to the Yankees, Hinch put the ball in McCullers' hands for Game 4.

"It's a big game for us. It's a big game for the team," said McCullers, who threw three innings of three-hit, two-run ball in Game 3 of the ALDS against Boston at Fenway Park, striking out four and walking two on 49 pitches. "Yankees have a great home record and are a great team. And we do the job putting ourselves in the situation, getting up 2–0. We knew it was going to be hard-fought innings, hard-fought games. It's a big situation to be able to pitch in, put us within a game of the World Series."

The son of a Yankee—McCullers' father, Lance, threw in 63 games for New York in 1989 and 1990—did his job on October 17 before 48,804 at Yankee Stadium. Six-plus innings, one run, two hits, and three strikeouts on 81 pitches. It was 4–0 Astros after the top of the seventh, and a 3–1 ALCS lead was within sight.

"He was awesome," Hinch said. "Really proud of him because I know how important this start was for him. He has had an up-and-down season, but who can top the first half?...A very difficult second half for him, and not knowing he was going to be in the rotation, his first relief outing in Boston. And then to come up and pitch with a ton of heart, really one mistake, the last pitch of his outing. I'm not even sure it was a mistake—Judge has done that a couple of times this year. Really, really proud of him. I thought he threw tremendously well."

The "mistake" to Judge—finally heating up and hitting .444 during the three games in Yankee Stadium—sent an 85-mph curveball 427 feet to center field. McCullers' 81st pitch of the night became his last, as Hinch turned to the Astros' bullpen (Chris Devenski, Joe Musgrove, Giles, Luke Gregerson) to finish the evening. A 4–0 Astros lead heading into the bottom of the seventh became a 6–4 meltdown, as New York scored all six of its runs in its final two frames at the plate.

Hinch was again left to defend a playoff pitching change after an Astros loss. "Chris Devenski is really good against left-handed hitters," he said. "At the beginning of the game, we definitely had plans for Devo getting that pocket. I think coming in, [Didi] Gregorius falling behind him and then getting the base hit set up the whole inning, and then the walk to Bird. Bird's a good hitter, he laid off a couple of tough change-ups. We just didn't get the results we wanted. We had the matchup we wanted."

The bigger problem for the Astros was their bats. They had ended up with four runs in Game 4, but three came in one inning, and they only totaled three hits. The series was even, but New York now had momentum, and the Astros had struggled at the plate since the ALCS began. "Their pitching lineup is really good," Hinch said. "They're throwing some good guys out there. And we've come up with some big hits—maybe not enough to feel like we're at our best. There's a little bit of anxiousness, but I'm not sure too many people play in October without a little bit of anxiousness."

Meanwhile, Judge was finding his balance at the plate, and the Yankees' hitters were locking in at home. Judge went 3-for-6, with two home runs, five RBIs, and two walks during Games 3 and 4, while New York totaled 14 runs and 15 hits in the initial two games at Yankee Stadium. The most powerful hitting team in baseball was cracking wood again, and New York's fans were witnessing another mid-series playoff turnaround.

"It was special again tonight. Every home game has been special," Girardi said. "I just feel like the fans are back. And I see things that I haven't seen in a while, and it reminds me a lot when I was playing here. So it's been fun to watch."

Game 5 was miserable for the team that, by the time it was over, was suddenly down to its last defeat of 2017.

It was set up as a bailout. Keuchel back on the mound at Yankee Stadium. The Astros needing just one victory in New York to carry a 3–2 ALCS lead back to Houston. The club with 101 regular-season wins returning to form now that the series had been evened, then clinching a spot in the World Series in its home city.

But it ended up 5–0 Yankees. The Astros only recorded four hits and never scored a run, while Keuchel only lasted $4^2/3$ innings, giving up seven hits and four runs. Reddick, Altuve, and Bregman went 0-for-4, as Tanaka rebounded from a tough Game 1 loss to throw seven innings of shutout ball. By the time the Astros were returning to Houston, the best-hitting team in baseball had reached a breaking point at the plate. They had been blown out, shut out, and had collapsed in New York. They were hitting .147 as a team in the ALCS and were pressing like it was the start of the 2016 season all over again.

"It's rare, because of how much offense we put up through the first six months of the season and even in the Division Series," Hinch said. "We've swung the bats very well and to this day I believe we're one good game coming out of it. We're going to go home. We hit well. We get a day off tomorrow, which is probably the most important thing, and try to make some offensive adjustments. The playoffs…if they get you to crack a little bit outside of your game plan, then they've got you. We haven't stayed in our game plan quite well enough to make adjustments."

Even with the slide, Hinch's public persona—on the field, in the dugout, behind a microphone—was a portrait of calm. Stay in the present. Let go of the past. Win today and do not waste time worrying about what cannot be changed. "Those games are behind us, so there's no real reason to look back now. They're in the books," said Hinch, during an October 19 off day that separated Game 5 in New York and Game 6 in Houston. "All we really need to focus on is the game at hand. Our guys are good at that. I think we have to deal with a lot this time of year, obviously, and as the series and the emotion goes along. We've said from the beginning it's a seven-game series. So I guess we really meant it, based on how it's turned out. We want it to be a seven-game series to get us to the next level."

Before the Astros left Yankee Stadium, ex-Yankees Beltran and McCann led a team meeting. Beltran would only hit .083 with four strikeouts in 12 ALCS at-bats. McCann would finish 3-for-16 with five strikeouts. But a team that entered New York more confident than ever was now shell-shocked and stunned, after dropping three straight games by a combined score of 19–5. The veteran presence that the Astros had intentionally added during the off-season made its biggest impact to date in late October, with the Astros' season officially on the line.

"I always try to make them aware of how blessed it is to have this opportunity when you get to play in a playoff in October. It doesn't happen very often," said Beltran, before Game 3. "The fact that it's happening for us, we have to embrace the moment, try to take advantage and try to use the platform to do something special for the organization, for themselves....I try to pass on to them that it's fun. Yes, it's a lot of pressure. But at the end of the day, you have to be able to manage your emotions, be able to go out there and do whatever you have to do."

The Astros needed to loosen up again. They also needed two wins to stay alive in 2017.

14

HE PUT US ON HIS BACK

It's not easy to get here. And I don't take any of this for granted, and this is what we play for. These are the experiences that you remember at the end of your career when you look back, winning these games, just playing the World Series. Hopefully winning the World Series. It's a special bond that you create with that team and that city. It's really special for me to be a part of that and to be a part of that so quickly. I think I've been here for, somebody said like 50 days now. So to feel this bonded to a team and a city that quickly, I think is something special.

—Astros pitcher Justin Verlander

THERE WAS ONE advantage to being down 3–2 in the American League Championship Series to the New York Yankees: the Astros were handing the ball to their ace. Justin Verlander hadn't disappointed yet, and the 34-year-old right-hander had become the best pitcher in baseball since joining Houston's team August 31.

"When we wake up tomorrow morning we know we have an incredible opportunity to win," Astros manager A.J. Hinch said. "Justin Verlander is on the mound. It doesn't matter: Game 1, Game 6, a game on a Tuesday in July, August, September. So that's a good feeling. He raises the bar. Guys are going to want to do extra. We're going to have to fight that emotion....His presence will immediately make everybody sit up straight, stand up a little bit more, have a little bit more energy, because of the presence that he brings. It's hard to measure. It's hard to fake. You either have it or you don't. Verlander has it."

José Altuve and Aaron Judge both had it during the ALCS. For six months, the Astros second baseman and New York outfielder had battled for the AL MVP award. Then Altuve soared at the start of the playoffs, Judge swung through everything, and Astros fans were reminded of why they had pushed hard for Altuve all season.

Altuve dominated Games 1 and 2 of the ALCS—old-school hustle and an infield single to start it all, then sprinting from first to home for an earsplitting walkoff and 2–0 series lead—just like he hit almost everything in sight in the ALDS against the fading Red Sox. Judge finally came to life in Game 3 of the ALCS, setting up a three-game rally by New York that had the Yankees just one win away from their 41st World Series appearance and first since 2009. As Game 6 approached, the heart and soul of Hinch's Astros and the rookie slugger that Joe Girardi always stood behind had shined in a back-and-forth series now tilting toward New York.

Of course, Altuve being Altuve, he shined the spotlight toward Judge when the MVP debate resumed in real life. "Yet another reason why José Altuve is a perfect player," Hinch said. "He's humble in his own accomplishments and very complimentary of others. I will always back José Altuve. I think in this regard, I got to tell him he's wrong: José Altuve's the MVP. I'm biased. I love Aaron Judge and José Ramirez and Mike Trout, and the seasons that those guys had, but José was the most consistent player in the big leagues.... Offense, defense, base running—just the 'it' factor that he comes with every single day. He's the best hitter in the game, he leads the league virtually every year. We take 200 hits for granted, we take batting titles for granted around here now."

As his team slumped in Games 3 through 5, though, Altuve also fell off at the plate. Like the Astros, his strike zone expanded, and he entered Game 6 batting .278 (5-for-18) in the ALCS, following a scorching .533 (8-for-15) ALDS run.

By Game 3 in New York, Judge had regained his power stroke, reminding the baseball world that he was defined by much more than just playoff strikeouts. Entering Game 6, his .313 average in the ALCS ranked second on the Yankees, while he led the team with two homers, six RBIs, and 13 total bases. "I get a chance to play baseball every day. I get to live my dream," said Judge, who hit .284 with 52 home runs, 114 RBIs, 128 runs, and a 1.049 OPS during the regular season. "So you've got to take the ups with the downs. You can't have all the good, come out here and hit 1.000, even though I want to. It's baseball. I've got to enjoy the good times and the bad times. That's what I picked up and learned from my teammates. They've supported me through the good times and the bad times. Like I said, I get a chance to play in the ALCS with the New York Yankees, it's a dream come true."

Judge's improved plate discipline and game-by-game evolution in the box—battling the Astros' arms and refusing to settle at initial offerings—had Hinch praising the rookie before Game 6. "He's been good at hitting a couple of different pitches," he said. "I think his ability to stay grounded in the batter's box and not overswing has been very evident in this series. He's hit every pitch, whether it's been an up-and-in pitch, a breaking ball from [Lance] McCullers, a slider—these are really, really good pitches that don't normally get hit by anyone. And also it's been a weakness of his throughout the season. These adjustments that he's made have made it tough to go to an area inside the strike zone to get an out. He's as dangerous as anyone. He can mishit balls and carry them out of the ballpark."

Back inside the Astros' stadium after three losses in New York, Verlander acknowledged that earlier in his career he had taken for granted the opportunities—regular playoff appearances, being surrounded by All-Star talent—that many pro players never get to experience. "You almost think it's just easy and it will always be that way. I've learned that that's obviously not the case," Verlander said. "We had a guy, Sean Casey, joined our [Detroit Tigers] team when I was a rookie, and I was so shocked when he told me his whole career he'd never been in the playoffs, not even in the play-offs at all. That really surprised me. I always remember him saying that."

Detroit went 95–67 in 2006, knocking off the Yankees and Oakland Athletics in the playoffs, before falling to the St. Louis Cardinals in the World Series. Eleven years later, Verlander was taking the ball for the Astros in Game 6 of the ALCS against the Yankees at Minute Maid Park. If his new team was going to survive for one more day in 2017, their new ace would have to carry the Astros again.

"Obviously, I know this is one of the main reasons I was brought here," Verlander said. "I think so far I've done what they've asked or what they've needed of me to help the rotation and help get deep in the playoffs. This is obviously the biggest game for the Astros up to this point for this season. The expectations are there. My teammates, I'm sure, are expecting a lot of me. And I expect a lot of myself. So this is why we play the game. And I love these opportunities to pitch in these atmospheres, these type of games. It should be a lot of fun."

It was seven more innings of brilliance from No. 35. In the big-gest, most critical game of an already thrilling season, Verlander was playoff perfection once again. With the Astros, the team that wanted and needed him: a perfect 9–0 with 67 strikeouts and a surreal 1.23 ERA. In the ALCS against the Yankees: 16 innings, 21 strikeouts, one earned run. In career elimination-game playoff starts: 4–1 with 41 strikeouts and a 1.21 ERA.

After a 7–1 takedown of New York in Game 6, Verlander had two of the Astros' three victories in the ALCS and four playoff wins in 2017. "He's been everything that we could have hoped for and more," said Hinch, after Verlander held the Yankees score-less through seven innings, striking out eight and only allowing five hits on 99 pitches (70 strikes). "This guy prepares. He rises to the moment. He's incredibly focused, locked in during games, and emptied his tank tonight. And I'm so proud of him because I know how much it means to him. I know how much he puts into these outings. He chose to come here for games like this and beyond. We hope we all get to see him pitch again."

Brian McCann broke through, going 2-for-4 with an RBI double in the fifth, which broke open up a scoreless game and finally snapped the Astros out of their ALCS hitting slump. Altuve went 2-for-4 with three RBIs, clubbing his fourth home run of the postseason. George Springer leapt toward the roof near the 404-foot mark in center field at the perfect time. Carlos Correa and Yuli Gurriel answered Judge's solo shot in the eighth inning with back-to-back hits, as the Astros' bats locked in for the first time during the series.

"I'm not going to lie to you, it's a lot of emotions in that clubhouse. After this game, it was a crazy game," Altuve said. "But personally I really like the way we play in these kind of games, with everybody up. I believe in my team. Tomorrow [Game 7] is going to be a good night."

Just like Game 2 of the ALCS—124 pitches, nine old-school innings, 13 strikeouts for Verlander—Hinch's club would not have captured a win-or-end Game 6 and moved one step closer toward the Fall Classic without No. 35. Verlander became the first pitcher in baseball history with three consecutive scoreless starts in elimination games and had not allowed a run in 24 straight innings during elimination starts. With his team winning elimination game No. 1 and now just one victory away from the World Series, Verlander's run with the Astros had become one of the greatest for the franchise since major league baseball arrived in Houston in 1962.

"There's no point in saving anything," Verlander said. "And I think that's, again, why you can—I talked about forgetting what inning it is and not knowing where we are at in the game, how many pitches I have, or who's up. It's just kind of, I'm out there until I'm not out there any longer. And so in season, you sometimes...get deep in the game here, let me try to save some pitches. In a playoff, that's out the window, specifically in a 0–0 ballgame in a decisive game. So when it came down to it that sixth and seventh, back-to-back, I mean it really did, it took a lot out of me, especially kind of back-to-back stressful innings like that. And for me, my focus—when I look back at the 3–2 slider to [Aaron] Hicks was probably the pitch of the game for me. You could look at it and say the 3–0 slider to [Gary] Sanchez, but there were two outs in that situation. To Hicks, 3–2 there, if I don't execute that and he takes it or you know, worse, then it's a totally different ballgame."

All the trade rumors and prospects-for-an-October-ace questions that surrounded the Astros for months during the slow build-up toward the final trade deadline on August 31? Perfect hindsight on October 20. Verlander was exactly what the Astros had needed. A mound artist, stopper, and powerhouse throwback—and a reliever—who had thrown his new team into a Game 7 for just the second time in franchise history.

"For me to watch that, for everybody to watch that, those two performances—and after the first one he threw, the complete game—you don't see every day that a guy goes out in a tight game like that, just get better as the game goes on," said Charlie Morton, who was now set to take the mound for the Astros in the ALCS finale. "That's rare. And he's special. He's one of the greatest pitchers of our generation."

Game 2 against New York had felt like the peak point for Verlander. In Game 6 Verlander just gave and kept giving—for the 43,179 so proud to have him in orange and blue, for the 2017 Astros and the Game 7 that could send them all the way to the World Series. The Astros had six wins in the playoffs—Verlander had four of them. With each victory, he set the bar higher and tied himself to a city that could now almost feel the Fall Classic.

"It's pretty amazing to me how quickly these fans have bonded to me. And vice versa," Verlander said. "I feel it, I appreciate it, especially on the field. But around town, everybody is just wishing good luck. A fresh face, people—a lot of times in new cities, if they're not baseball fans they might not recognize me. But it seems like a lot of people here, they're involved and they want this team to win and they always come up and give me their blessing and want me to know they care, and that means a lot."

Game 7 of the ALCS set up Game 7 of the World Series.

Morton and McCullers on the mound. The Astros' bats coming through early. The bullpen holding on and doing its job, as the opposing team gradually realized that the best team was on the other side of the field.

The Astros ended CC Sabathia's night after just $3\frac{1}{3}$ innings, while every batter in Hinch's lineup recorded at least one hit and the Astros' Core Four went a combined 5-for-15. As Evan Gattis and McCann steadied the bottom of the order, Morton and McCullers combined for a three-hit shutout that featured 11 total strikeouts and curve after curve from McCullers.

"We go to New York and get beat up and come back, and needing some big-time performances, and we got it in both games, specifically today with Morton and McCullers," Hinch said. "We couldn't ask for it to map out any better. These guys came out throwing strikes, quality strikes—power breaking balls work against these guys. They executed a great game plan. Brian McCann handled them terrifically to come up with some big hits. And we look up and we got our 27 outs from two guys. Everybody talks about Game 7, you're going to need 12 pitchers to get through 27 outs. Outside of a couple times, I warmed Will Harris up about half a dozen times. And [Ken] Giles at the end. We were perfectly content with what Morton and McCullers were doing, because they were so dominant."

So were the Astros throughout Game 7. They took a 1–0 lead in the fourth, added three runs in the fifth and never let the Yankees breathe. Morton and McCullers, two names that entered the 2017 season surrounded by question marks, were the perfect answer for the Astros in a win that sent them to the World Series. It was 3–2 New York in the ALCS, heading back to Houston. Then Verlander, Morton, and McCullers brought the Astros their second World Series appearance in 56 seasons. The Astros outscored the Yankees 11–1 in the final two ALCS games at Minute Maid Park, silencing the most-powerful lineup in the sport.

"You've got to give them credit," Girardi said. "They pitched their rear ends off. And the bottom line is, they beat us."

After 101 wins and in the year of Hurricane Harvey, Houston's Astros were in the World Series. They had beat the storied Red Sox and Yankees to claim the American League pennant, outpunching Boston in the Fenway Park rain, then fighting off two elimination games to take down New York. When Game 7 of the ALCS was over, Minute Maid Park's roof opened to show off downtown Houston, while "American League Champions 2017" remained locked on the big board.

Gattis had gone deep. Hit-everything Altuve had, too. Ric Flair introduced it all on the big screen in the season of woos. And when McCann lined a two-run double in a three-run fifth, 43,201 screaming fans inside the ballpark knew exactly what was coming: the Astros versus the Los Angeles Dodgers for the 2017 World Series title. A rebuilt baseball team was heading for a world stage.

"The standards that have been established here, the work that's been put in, the synergy that goes on from the front office to the clubhouse, from ownership," Hinch said. "We really are connected because we all have a common goal, and that's to win. And I don't care whether you're old school, new school, analytical, traditional, it's about winning at this level. And I think this organization gets it."

Five years prior, owner Jim Crane and general manager Jeff Luhnow had brought out the wrecking ball, deconstructing and rebuilding everything in sight. In 2013 the Astros lost a franchise-record 111 games, won only 51, and were officially the worst club in team history. "Who are these guys?" was the only popular refrain at near-empty Minute Maid Park. Giving away good tickets was almost impossible. Even discussing the laughingstock Lastros on local talk radio was forbidden.

Twelve years after the Astros were blanked 4–0 by the world champion Chicago White Sox, the even-better 2017 Astros were returning to the Fall Classic. They were led by Verlander and Dallas Keuchel at the top of their rotation, possessed the deepest lineup in the game, and had already knocked off two of the most-respected franchises in pro sports. At worst, the Astros were winning the pennant in 2017. At best, they were also taking down the Dodgers and would end up as world champs.

"Keep the high," said Verlander, who was named the ALCS MVP. "We played two win-or-go-home games and we won them. I've been on the other side of this twice, where I was part of the World Series team that had swept and won early and was waiting to see who we were going to play, and the other teams went deep in their series. This team is playing great baseball. We played our best baseball when our backs were against the wall. And I think when you're battle-tested coming into the last series, I think you just try to maintain that feeling."

As the roar continued inside the Astros' soaked clubhouse, Hinch spoke of a "singular focus." His 2017 team had entered spring training believing it could be the best in baseball. They were now guaranteed at least four more games. And while many were already expecting the team with the highest payroll in major league baseball to claim the last series of the year, Hinch's Astros knew they could compete with—and beat—anyone in the sport on any stage.

The rebuilt Astros were in the World Series. And they were still ahead of schedule.

"There's some guys in the clubhouse who were here during the build and then obviously we've gotten close along the way with the 2015 playoffs," Hinch said. "And then feeling good about our team last year, falling short. And then this year getting the division title…and now the World Series. So I have such an appreciation—I never knew what it felt like to get to the World Series in any job I've had in 20 years, and now I do. And I have a great appreciation for what it takes to run this journey. We won 100-plus games in the regular season. We won a lot of games in the postseason, so far. But it's not easy. This is a grind and getting through so many ups and downs regardless of how the season goes is awesome when you get rewarded with a chance to win a world championship."

Clayton Kershaw, Justin Turner, Yasiel Puig, and the flashy, high-priced Dodgers were waiting.

Altuve, Springer, Correa, Bregman, Verlander, Keuchel—the Astros—were flying to Los Angeles for the World Series.

15

IF YOU LIKE
OCTOBER BASEBALL

It's so easy in this game to get down, especially when—I mean, we have the TV on before the games. You see everyone saying how great this Dodger bullpen is and how our offense hasn't been going. It's so easy to say, "Man, we're probably not going to win this game, down two against one of the best bullpens in baseball."...I guess maybe that was just my message, is stay positive. Remember how good you are and just play the game. It's only two runs. This team, since I've been here—and I know it hasn't been that long—but two runs is nothing. And all of a sudden two runs seemed like it was the Grand Canyon. And I just kind of—I don't even know if anybody heard me, but I was just trying to remind these guys two runs is nothing.

—Justin Verlander

THE DIRT BEHIND first base and third filled up with stacked video cameras and glaring lights. A portable stage rolled toward second base in sweltering heat. Security personnel guarded every entrance, constantly checking for official passes and only letting the right people through. It was the day before the Los Angeles Dodgers hosted the Houston Astros at Dodger Stadium in Game 1 of the 2017 World Series. It looked like a real-life movie set.

Never mind that the Dodgers were more than three hours away from taking the field, and media day inside a revered stadium—which features palm trees and a mountain as an unofficial backdrop—was just a fake walk-through for the real thing. After 162 regular-season games, wild-card matchups, and two playoff rounds, major league baseball's big show had arrived in L.A.

"This is the hardest part," said ex-Astro Enrique "Kiké" Hernández, who was four victories away from winning the World Series with his 104-win team. "But, obviously, this is L.A. and it's kind of crazy at all times. We need to figure out a way to deal with the noise, as we like to say."

The team from the fourth-largest city in America was obviously good enough to win it all. But on an international sports stage, and in a city that makes a very good living off make-believe, the Dodgers were the movie. The Astros were the trailer—until they won one and actually made it a series.

"Houston's never won a World Series game. We plan to change that very soon," Astros general manager Jeff Luhnow said.

Getting a decent, up-close look at the best team in baseball was a physical challenge during the media circus that preceded Game 1. A small room was used to contain Los Angeles' entire roster, which left some of the Dodgers' biggest names surrounded by media circles running 10 deep. When the Astros finally arrived for their show in the same room, the majority of cameras and eyes were glued to the field, watching the highest payroll in baseball field soft grounders and stand in the outfield.

"You know what? The city of L.A.'s a big city," Astros closer Ken Giles said. "They're a big-market team. They have a lot of great experiences and a lot of great players. Of course, they're going to look like they're going to overshadow us a little bit. But that's reality."

But were the 101-win Astros—American League pennant winners representing a city still recovering from Hurricane Harvey—being overlooked in Hollywood? "Not at all," said veteran catcher Brian McCann, who spent time in New York before joining A.J. Hinch's team. "We feel very good coming into this series and very confident."

What about underdogs?

"I know what you're saying," McCann said. "But not one bit. Not one bit."

Inside Dodger Stadium, where almost everything is colored Dodger blue and white, major league history covered the corridors. Six titles and 31 playoff appearances in 134 seasons for the historic franchise. Glass-covered walls loaded with Cy Young Awards, Gold Gloves, a 1988 World Series trophy, and jerseys once belonging to Sandy Koufax, Don Drysdale, and so many more.

For the Astros, making their fifth League Championship Series was a big deal less than two weeks ago. To win the World Series for the first time in franchise history, Hinch's club would have to take down the Boston Red Sox, New York Yankees, and Los Angeles Dodgers in one unbelievable month. The rebuilt Astros already believed in themselves. If they took four wins from Los Angeles, the rest of baseball finally would, too.

"From the first week of April to the end of September, I felt top to bottom we were the best team," said lefthander Dallas Keuchel, who was set to face lefty Clayton Kershaw in Game 1. "I give tremendous credit to Cleveland for winning 22....But it took a 22-...game winning streak to even catch us in the standings. When you take a step back and look at that, that means we were playing really well....Personally, I thought we were the best team from start to finish, and I thought the Dodgers were the best team in the National League start to finish. So this is going to be a great matchup. And it's not overblown because we've both won a hundred games. It really is, top to bottom—pitching staffs, bullpens, pinch-runners, you name it, coaching staffs—it really is, top to bottom, the two best teams."

It became one of the best World Series in baseball history. And for a 31-year-old backup catcher/designated hitter from Dallas, Texas, the Fall Classic was a lifetime dream come true before it even began.

Evan Gattis was never supposed to make it this far and had already led multiple lives. The janitor's identification card that served as his Twitter photo said it all. As does the man who blasted a 405-foot home run to open up Game 7 of the ALCS also having car valet, ski-lift operator, and pizza cook on his résumé. Children and adults dream of playing in the World Series millions upon millions of times. There was a time in Gattis' unorthodox career path when reaching baseball's grandest stage was the last thought in his mind. "I still can't believe it. I can't believe it. This is a dream come true," said Gattis, who hit .400 in the Astros' ALDS win against Boston and ignited the ALCS clincher against the Yankees. "I'm grateful to be on a team and in an organization this good. Making it to the pinnacle of baseball, it still hasn't set in, and it's an incredible opportunity. You try to every minute take a step back and kind of appreciate it from a different light."

Gattis spent all seven World Series games allowing the moment to soak in. Thanks to Keuchel hitting ninth in Game 1, there was no place for the third-year Astro in Hinch's initial lineup. But on the "Can you believe he's in the World Series?" meter, Gattis topped everyone in orange and Dodger blue.

In his youth, Gattis caught Kershaw during a Perfect Game tournament. Both were from Dallas and crossed paths during travel ball. "I knew he had some life," Gattis said. "I just couldn't predict what his fastball was going to do. I don't know if he could at the time....It's cool to look back. I mean, this is a boys' game."

Gattis eventually burned out on baseball, though, and later battled depression, drugs, and suicidal thoughts. Even after he rediscovered his childhood passion for the sport that has now made his name, it still took a stay at the University of Texas of the Permian Basin (Odessa) just to be drafted during the 23rd round in 2010.

Baseball being baseball and life being life, Gattis' third season with Astros had not gone exactly as expected. He led the team with a career-high 32 home runs in 2016, which followed a career year in 2015, when Gattis played in 153 of 162 games and became a critical piece (27 homers, 88 RBIs) on the club's first playoff run in a decade. To get to 101 wins in 2017, several Astros had to make sacrifices. Marwin González was so good he kept forcing his way into Hinch's daily lineup. But Gattis had to split time with Carlos Beltran at DH and McCann at catcher—a position Gattis reaccustomed himself to in 2015. The fifth-year pro was limited to just 84 games and 300 at-bats for the second-best team in Astros history. But in the ALDS and World Series, Gattis would again swing a critical bat for his team.

"He's had to fit in a little differently than last year. And he's accepted it while continuing to be hungry to want more," Hinch said. "He's not a complainer. He does his job. There's always a sense that he can do more, and it's absolutely true....He's deserved more at-bats than I've given him, yet he hasn't really let that affect his mental preparation."

Did Gattis still think about his old life, when he intentionally left the game behind? "It's my story. Everybody's got a story," he said. "Everybody remembers where they were when they were 20 or 25 or whatever. It's just very much a part of my life." So was walking onto the Dodger Stadium infield and proudly lining up with his Astros, standing feet away from an oversized "World Series 2017" logo, the American flag stretched across the entire outfield. Four planes cut through the sky after the national anthem was belted. Gattis and his Astros were just four wins away from a championship, going for it all in 2017.

"To be a world champion in anything would be incredible," he said.

World Series—the words and logo were everywhere. Patches on everything. T-shirts only bearing letters and numbers—WS 2017— but meaning so much to so many. Houston's Astros were in the World Series for just the second time since 1962. An entire city and its fan base were carried cross-country to famous Dodger Stadium by Hinch's American League pennant–winning club. Now that the Astros had arrived, could they handle life on baseball's biggest stage, and all the pressure and attention that came with it?

"The schedule is pretty crazy, just because of the emotions," Hinch said. "I don't think any of us allowed ourselves to pack until we knew we needed to pack. Just the superstitious side of all of us. But it was a whirlwind, obviously the celebration after Game 7 (of the ALCS), just the emotion that goes into it. And obviously we left the next day. Got here last night. And then you're trying to hurry and prep for a team that you rarely see. We'll take it. The fatigue or the uncertainty of the game plans and stuff like that, we'll spend for the next 24 hours. But what a range of emotions and just pure joy and appreciation for being here and kind of general excitement. Your body feels pretty good right now, even though we know what time of the year it is."

The day before he faced Kershaw in stifling heat, Keuchel was asked to reflect on being a part of the 111-loss Astros in 2013, then starting Game 1 of the World Series just four years later. He had constantly thought of the franchise's turnaround, so the magnitude of what the Astros had already accomplished was not lost on a Cy Young Award winner who went a combined 9–18 during his initial two pro seasons on 100-plus-loss teams.

"When you're pretty much at an open tryout at the end of 2012—when we traded away a bunch of the veteran guys that we still had left, into 2013—a lot of the guys didn't take advantage or weren't really serious about it," Keuchel said. "It was like they were handed stuff and they thought they were going to be the next greatest player. And for myself, I started out well my first four or five starts, but really faltered, and I knew if I was going to make a name for myself or stick in the big leagues, that I needed to make some adjustments. And Marwin, José [Altuve], and myself are the only ones left from 2012, 2013. And they appreciate every day just as much as I do....It's one of the most special things when at nighttime I'm thinking about, we're going to the World Series, and just…four years ago we were going home the last day of the season. And it was like, thank goodness, the season is over with."

Baseball's daily pull returned to Houston during the thrill of 2015, when the Astros made the playoffs for the first time in a decade. With the city's team in the World Series for just the second time in 56 seasons, Houston was united around one shared love. To the people who had devoted so much of their own lives to the city's baseball team—a groundskeeper, a bullpen catcher, a longtime announcer—another trip to the Fall Classic was life-changing.

"We talk all the time about players that come and go, and maybe players that have been through the lean years," Hinch said. "But there's a lot of employees here who rode the journey along, as well."

The Astros' first World Series appearance in 2005 had been defined by the smallest of margins. Yes, Craig Biggio, Jeff Bagwell, Lance Berkman, Roger Clemens, and company were swept by the Chicago White Sox. But two of the games were decided by just one run, all four were close, and Game 3 required 14 innings for a victor. Four World Series losses had come down to six extra runs for the White Sox, and Geoff Blum—who had two stints with the Astros as a player and was a TV analyst for the 2017 team—had tilted the series to Chicago with a 14th-inning, go-ahead homer for the White Sox in Game 3. So close, but so far away.

Game 1 of the 2017 World Series felt like a repeat of 2005, and a painful reminder of why the Astros had always fallen under baseball's brightest lights in previous years. The first pitch Los Angeles saw in the 2017 World Series suddenly became a 1–0 Dodgers lead, as Chris Taylor crushed an 88-mph fastball from Keuchel. In the sixth Justin Turner followed a Taylor walk with another no-doubter, and really, that was it in the L.A. night. Dodgers 3–1 in Game 1 and three wins away from being World Series champions.

"They had two big swings, we had one. They had a walk before one of their big swings, it's 3–1....It's no more complicated than that," Hinch said. "It's tough. It's a tough lead when you go up against Kershaw. But it's going to be a tough lead when you go against [Justin] Verlander. Keuchel was really good tonight. He was just a pitch or two less than Kershaw. He wasn't as fancy with the punch-outs. But take nothing away from these guys, it was a well-pitched game on both sides."

Alex Bregman lifted a 1–1 Kershaw fastball into left field, tying the game at 1 in the fourth. Dodger Stadium, which pounded and shook almost the entire evening, was temporarily silenced. But Kershaw killed the Astros, striking out 11 on just 83 pitches, while the American League's best team only managed three hits and barely threatened at the plate.

"This team is a really good hitting team. They hit a lot of homers and don't strike out. There's little room for error," Kershaw said. "So it's important for me to establish pitches, be able to throw multiple things for strikes, and thankfully I was able to do that tonight. I made a few mistakes, obviously Bregman got me, then threw one down the middle to Correa that he popped up—that could've gone a long way, too. So for the most part, though, I'll take it."

The slimmest of margins, the smallest things—just like 2005. The Astros fell to 0–5 all-time in the Fall Classic, and had lost all five games by just eight combined runs.

Hollow, overeager bats had been a problem since Game 3 of the ALDS for the Astros. But Hinch's team was also just a couple hits away from a Game 1 victory in the World Series, and had yet to hand the ball to its ace. "These are pretty damn good teams. Both 100-win teams," Hinch said. "Bregman put a good swing on the ball. We had some other pretty good swings. But you don't give in, you also don't get much. And I think playoff baseball, World Series baseball, would you expect anything less than a margin about the size of one swing?"

When Turner doubled down on the Dodgers' power, destroying a 1–2, 87-mph pitch to suddenly make it 3–1 home team in the sixth, L.A. knew it had enough. A crowd of 54,253 screamed, "Justin! Justin! Justin!" while Dodgers relievers Brandon Morrow and Kenley Jansen combined for two innings of hitless relief to back up Kershaw's seven-inning dominance.

"Loud. It was loud. That was probably just as loud as it was on the [NLCS Game 2] walkoff homer," said Turner, who reached a Dodgers postseason record 14 RBIs. "This place was the most electric I've ever seen it, which it should be—the first World Series here in 29 years. Our fans are fired up. They're pumped. The buzz around the city is crazy. And obviously we're all excited to be able to let them enjoy this with us."

Taylor and Turner combined for two home runs, three runs, and three RBIs to ignite the Dodgers. The Astros' 1–7 hitters only totaled two hits, which was set up by a backward start for leadoff hitter George Springer. After hitting .412 in the ALDS, Springer had fallen to .115 in the ALCS against the Yankees, striking out seven times in 26 at-bats. He began the World Series even worse, going 0-for-4 with four strikeouts and anxiously hacking at air—tossing his bat away after one particularly filthy Kershaw K—while the Astros' Core Four went a combined 2-for-15.

During his postgame press conference, a tenser-than-normal Hinch linked "must-win" with Game 2 before a reporter did. "I anticipated the whole must-win question, which you didn't say it, but I did," he said. "But every game is sort of a must-win. I wanted to get out of here with a sweep, and now that's not going to happen."

Then Hinch was asked if he would consider moving down Springer. The highly athletic center fielder rivaled Altuve as the heart and soul of the Astros. When the team was at its best, Springer was often the sparkplug that fired up the machine. During Game 1, Springer was clearly trying to do too much, all at once. Hinch responded by backing the Astro whose 2014 debut had marked the beginning of a new era for the franchise. "He'll be leading off," Hinch said. "He had a tough night at work, and a lot of our guys did. I know George has struggled. If he hits the first pitch tomorrow into the gap or hits a single or hits the ball out of the ballpark, you'd be amazed how good he feels."

One instantly historic game later, it would become one of the most important decisions of the Astros' unbelievable season.

Springer had helped inspire and set the tone for his team all season. But by publicly supporting the Astros' struggling leadoff hitter after a tough Game 1, Hinch sent a message to his squad. They had made it this far by being exactly who they were. Why back down now, just when their season was reaching its peak?

In Game 2, Springer reminded everyone why he was so special to the Astros. And his team proved once again that it was not backing down to anyone. It took 4 hours and 19 minutes to complete. It lasted 11 innings and featured eight home runs. It was 1–0 Astros heading into the bottom of the fifth, then 3–1 Dodgers after the sixth, mirroring the game-changing turnaround from Game 1. Then, just when it felt like the 2017 World Series had locked onto its final path—Los Angeles was just too strong and deep; the Astros once again were not ready for the national lights—Houston's baseball team pulled out a victory that instantly changed the series and perfectly set up the even-more-unbelievable magic of Game 5.

Springer went 3-for-5 with two RBIs and a walk in Game 2. His two-run home run in the 11th inning, blasted toward right-center field at 11:15 PM Houston time, became the biggest hit in Astros history—until it was topped four days later.

"Probably as nerve-wracking as it is in the stands for everybody else," Springer said. "You know who's on the other team, you know who's on deck, and you know who's hitting. And when that last out is made, you finally breathe. But that's an emotional high—emotional high to low to high again. But that's why we play the game. And that's the craziest game that I've ever played in, and it's only Game 2."

Game 2 was over. Then it was not. It was over again. Then life was suddenly rediscovered once again. The Astros created their own magic in the Hollywood night, stunning Dodger Stadium into silence, edging Los Angeles 7–6 in 11 innings and recording their first World Series win in franchise history.

"I've been part of some pretty exciting games," Verlander said. "But with all that this one entailed—to be in the World Series and to be down a game; the roller coaster of emotion. No, I mean, this is an instant classic. And to be able to be part of it is pretty special."

Dodgers utility man Kiké Hernández, who came up in the Astros farm system and played 24 games for the 92-loss 2014 club, made Dodger Stadium shake in the 10th after he hit a two-out RBI single to right field that tied the game at 5–5. But the Astros were big and grand enough for the world stage, crushing four huge, series-changing home runs—González, Altuve, Carlos Correa, and Springer—just in time.

"That's an incredible game on so many levels, so many ranges of emotion," Hinch said. "If you like October baseball—if you like any kind of baseball—that's one of the most incredible games you'll ever be a part of."

The Astros were up 1–0 after three, down 3–1 entering the eighth, down 3–2 entering the ninth, tied 3–3 after nine, then up 5–3 in the 10th and tied again, 5–5, heading into the 11th, before taking a 7–5 lead on Springer's two-run home run in the 11th, and holding on to win it by a final score of 7–6. Game 2 was a wild World Series battle that kept turning and changing and, for a while, just refused to end. All that was on the line: a 2–0 Dodgers World Series lead versus a Fall Classic tied up at 1–1, with Houston's ballclub returning home with a new jolt of life and three consecutive games at roaring Minute Maid Park.

"It's huge. I think the ability to win this game tonight, I mean, you can't quantify how much that means," Verlander said. "I mean, we play so well at home. These guys play so well at home....For everything to be going right for the Dodgers tonight, late into their bullpen and for us to come back and win that game, I mean, that's a game changer. That's huge. That's why I love this team. There's no quit, top to bottom of the lineup. Anybody can win a game at any time."

The Astros used five pitchers. The Dodgers turned to nine. Verlander began the game on fire. But for the first time since he became an Astro, he also looked a little human, giving up three runs off two hits and walking two in six innings. As the movie-like game unfolded, the Astros' ace became a public cheerleader for his team.

Verlander told González he was going to change the game. The super utility man soon kept the Astros alive, becoming the first player since Boston's Dwight Evans in 1975 to hit a game-tying home run on the road in the ninth inning of the World Series.

"I didn't think it was going to be a game-tying home run. I thought it was going to be a game-winning," Verlander said. "That's what I told him. I don't know if that's when the videos caught me popping out of the tunnel or not, I don't know when. I was kind of hiding. Obviously, it was extremely emotional. And I was in the exact same spot as George's home run because, why not? The inning before we scored a couple of runs, I'm going to be in the same spot. But, I mean, off the bat they're yelling 'Go!' It's an off-speed pitch that he hits opposite field. I mean, as long as I've been playing the game, you've got to hit that ball pretty good. So we're cheering for it. And as soon as it goes, we're in the video room. I almost fainted, I think, three times. I'm not joking. Cheering so loudly I had to take a minute to recompose myself so I didn't pass out."

Dreams were made of this. Seasons were ended and broken. Four pitches, four swings...and the World Series changes.

"These guys, they can do a lot of things, and they fight to the last out," Dodgers manager Dave Roberts said. "They play 27 outs. And that's the same thing we do."

It all began with a manager backing his player the night before. Hinch stood up for Springer, and Springer pushed his team over the top. "It's huge," Springer said. "Obviously, I didn't have the best game last night. And as a player you tend to know it and you press, and you want to do things that you can't do. And for [Hinch] to have my back and to say that, 'Hey, you're still going to hit first and you're still going to set the tone for us,' it slowed me down. I was doing things that I don't normally do. And for him to have my back, it means the world to me. And I'll always have his back. And that just shows who he is."

The Astros had scored three runs in the final two innings to erase the Red Sox at Fenway Park, then won two ALCS elimination games against the Yankees just to make the World Series. Games 1 and 2 of the Fall Classic had been decided by three runs, and the second contest had required 11 innings and more than four hours to complete. After the biggest home runs and victory in franchise history, the Astros were now presented with a clear path to their first world championship. Games 3–5 were back in Houston at Minute Maid Park, where Hinch's club was undefeated in the playoffs. Win two of them, and the Astros could be on their way toward a world title.

"[Game 2] was a pretty special game. Not only the first win for the Astros in World Series history, but just the way that it happened," said Lance McCullers Jr., who would take the ball in Houston for Game 3. "Our guys showed a lot of heart, showed we were a relentless group. So hats off to them, and they were swinging the bats, and the guys coming in doing their job....I'm excited. I feel really good. And I just have to continue to stick with my plan and stay in the moment."

A franchise that had previously never won a World Series game was finishing things the right way in 2017, rewriting accepted storylines and pushing Houstonians toward a word that normally broke their sporting hearts: *belief*. A team loaded with clutch bats and interchangeable stars had also shredded three of the best bullpens in baseball in series-changing moments: Game 4 of the ALDS, when Bregman went over the Green Monster off Chris Sale; then Josh Reddick and Carlos Beltran hit Craig Kimbrel to add their names to the list; Game 2 of the ALCS, when Altuve and Correa got to New York flamethrower Aroldis Chapman in the ninth for a joyous walkoff; then the instant classic, emotional roller-coaster that was Game 2 in Los Angeles, when the Astros clubbed four majestic homers in the final three frames to even the World Series at 1–1.

Game 1 came down to one more big hit for the richest team in MLB. Game 2 began with Vin Scully handing the ball to Fernando Valenzuela, and only ended when one side finally ran out of new heroes. If Yasiel Puig had been able to catch Bregman's looping liner in the eighth, the 101-win Astros were 99.9 percent likely to return home in a huge 2–0 hole against a 104-win team. Someone had also jumped into the Astros' bullpen, and there was a fire near the stadium. The battle for the world title was just beginning. The Astros were already preparing for an unpredictable series that kept changing paths.

"These series are long. I don't know why anyone would race to a conclusion, other than trying to be right faster," Hinch said. "You're usually going to be wrong if you make an assumption on anything, especially this time of year. These are two incredible teams that are going to fight. Seven-game series, you have to win four. We've each won one. It doesn't mean it's going to be over in five, but it could be. That's the reality of these series. We're not going to ride the emotion of hot, cold, and belief and non-belief. We're going to stay believing. We are going to worry about Friday night and take the rest of the series after that."

Believing in the Astros had been contagious at home. Hinch's team at Minute Maid Park during the playoffs: 6–0 with a .276 batting average, 10 home runs, .841 OPS, and 1.17 ERA. Away from Houston: 2–5 while hitting .219 with seven homers, a .654 OPS, and 6.30 ERA. "This is L.A.!" chants and pulsing techno music were about to be replaced by "MVP! MVP!" singalongs for Altuve and constant woos from a crowd wrapped in orange and blue.

"It's quite an environment. When we play under the roof, our fans get going. It was one of the loudest stadiums the last series. I expect it to be the same," Hinch said. "It is a great environment at home. I think that's what makes people feel good. We're coming off one of the most epic baseball games in any of our careers....So that feels good. It will feel good right up to first pitch and then it will be a new game. So I think our guys are ready."

Biggio had stood behind the Astros the entire time. Bagwell kept up with and loved watching the 2017 team, but mostly remained in the background when he was around. Biggio was up front, hands-on, and constantly present. The 2015 Baseball Hall of Fame inductee still bled for the Astros and took in as much as possible of the World Series up close. "This is the second time it's ever happened in the history of the organization," Biggio said. "To be able to enjoy this with them, I'm happy for them. I live through them. I'm excited for them. And we'll see—hopefully something good can happen."

When Hinch's club walked into the clubhouse before it tried to advance against the Yankees in the ALCS, Biggio pulled several Astros in close while Minute Maid Park was still filling up. When New York was silenced and Houston's baseball team was heading toward the Fall Classic, Biggio watched the clinching celebration near the main stage, then shared a huge smile and warm hug with Altuve.

"This organization, it's all he knows," Hinch said. "He lives in Houston. He's been a part of every process. The interview process for me as a manager, he was involved in. He's seen different owner-ship groups come through, different GMs come through. He's been a constant that the Houston Astros fans have been able to lean on. And having him be a participant in all this is really priceless."

Before the Hollywood drama of Game 2, Biggio leaned against a batting cage—wearing sunglasses, a jacket, and jeans—while the Astros were beginning to warm up. Within minutes, he held pri-vate conversations with McCann and Reddick, then moved on to everyone from owner Jim Crane and general manager Jeff Luhnow to 2016 world champion David Ross. Real MLB friendships still made a difference to Biggio.

"You can't just walk in there once or twice a year, thinking that you're going to be able to have a relationship," Biggio said. "Com-ing in every day and being around these guys, it takes a little bit of time to develop their trust. And if you develop people's trust, they'll open up and talk to you. The game changes. People change. And so for me, I've been loyal and dedicated to one city, one organization, and that's what I said in my Hall of Fame speech. To be able to give it back to an organization and give it back to a fan base...that's what it's about."

Even the eventual AL MVP made a point to thank Biggio for his constant dedication. "When I don't feel really good, he comes to me, makes me feel way better, and he brings me back the energy that I need to play," Altuve said.

Game 3 made the Astros feel even better. Two wins away from winning the World Series, and they still had not lost a home game since the playoffs began. Ex-Ranger Yu Darvish was battered and discarded before the second inning was over, while McCull-ers fought and battled for just long enough. There was a sudden four-run outbreak during the second inning and a critical Little League–like run in the fifth for the home team. It was Brad Peacock having McCullers' back, throwing $3^{2}/_{3}$ innings of hitless relief, as the Astros downed the Dodgers 5–3 and took a 2–1 series lead.

"Four runs in any game is big. Four runs in the World Series is huge," said Hinch, after an uneven contest that featured two Los Angeles errors and Darvish only lasting 1²/₃ innings. "To get that kind of momentum started—get the crowd into it, have a lead—puts a ton of pressure on the other dugout. Obviously the quality of our at-bats tonight was incredible. That's more of our identity. That's what we're about. And to see it carry over from the last game to this game was welcome."

The Astros racked up 12 hits to the Dodgers' four, led by a 3–9 attack that saw Altuve through McCann record at least one hit apiece. Yuli Gurriel and Reddick combined to go 4-for-9, and a second-inning homer by Gurriel—who later apologized for making a racially insensitive in-game gesture toward Darvish—pushed the Astros forward for the team's first home World Series win in franchise history.

"The good part of our lineup is that we can score from anywhere. And we have really good hitters up and down the lineup," Hinch said. "The bottom of our order, especially the big inning, we just put good at-bat after good at-bat after good at-bat....Wherever we are in the lineup, we feel we have a good chance to get on base early, and somebody behind him can drive him in. Yuli has been very good for us. He's a professional hitter who can hit any pitch, any count, any place in the ballpark. Getting us kickstarted today with a home run was huge."

Since the top of the ninth in Game 2 before a stunned Dodger Stadium crowd, the pennant winner from the American League had felt like the stronger and more driven team. Puig dropped things, bounced balls, and ran into outs. Springer dove into shallow center field for hero catches and hit a game-winning blast. After recording just one run and three hits in Game 1, the Astros broke out for 12 runs and 26 hits in back-to-back Fall Classic victories.

"Seeing the guys start swinging the bat like that again toward the end of the [second] L.A. game, you come home with a bunch of confidence," McCullers said. "Darvish is as good as it gets in this game, especially with all the pitches he throws and the command he throws it with. I think for the guys to just really zone in and battle out some awesome at-bats—to wait until they got their pitch to do some damage with—all the credit to those guys for putting up one heck of a game."

McCullers and Peacock were the strongest stories in Game 3. The latter impressed yet again—striking out four and only walking one in 3 2/3 scoreless innings—continuing a career season that began with an uncertain Opening Day roster spot. Los Angeles went deep into its bullpen again, using six arms. Hinch only needed two pitchers for a 2–1 advantage in the World Series.

"It was crazy....After the eighth, A.J. asked if I felt good," Peacock said. "I said, 'Yeah.' 'All right. You're going back out.' I'm shocked. I'm just glad he gave me the opportunity to do that. And it was a lot of fun out there, for sure."

It would not matter after the first day of November. But Game 4 was a blown opportunity for the Astros. The cracks seen in Game 3 of the ALDS and Games 3–5 of the ALCS—all Astros losses—reappeared. And on a night that began with so much potential, an increasingly unreliable bullpen let the team down again.

Morton smoothly fired through 6 1/3 innings of three-hit, one-run ball, striking out seven on 76 pitches (51 strikes). Springer blasted a solo shot into the Crawford Boxes, breaking up Alex Wood's no-hitter in the sixth. With the score 1–0 home team heading into the seventh—a potential 3–1 series lead with Game 5 back at Minute Maid Park—it suddenly became 6–2 Dodgers and another series tie.

"I let the team down," said Giles, who, through Game 4, had allowed five earned runs, four hits, and two walks in 1 2/3 World Series innings. It was 1–1 as the top of the ninth approached. But Los Angeles blew Game 4 apart with five runs, narrowing MLB's 2017 championship to a final best-of-three.

"We've got to go out there and try to take it," Astros shortstop Carlos Correa said. "Nobody is just going to give it to us. We've got to earn it and we've got to play better baseball in order for us to win these last two games."

After 15 playoff games, Hinch was still figuring out just how much he could trust his relievers. He had experimented with Verlander, Peacock, and McCullers out of the pen. Game 4 of the World Series was another reminder why the Astros' manager took all the alternate routes to reach nine postseason victories. Will Harris allowed L.A. to tie it in the seventh. Then Giles and Joe Musgrove proceeded to allow three hits, two walks, and five runs in a disastrous ninth.

"Obviously, it builds in the postseason because there's so much attention on these outs," Hinch said. "And when you're a back-end reliever, oftentimes—unless you're extraordinarily dominant—you're only talked about when you suffer, when you struggle."

Hinch turned to Giles in a still-tied ninth, when he could have stayed with Chris Devenski, who'd just thrown a hitless eighth. Game 4 then fell apart, and emptied-out Minute Maid Park was soon serenaded with ringing "Let's Go, Dodgers!" chants.

"They're all crappy pitches," Giles said. "Not where I want 'em. I need to do better. I need to pick up this team. I need to carry my weight."

Game 5—Kershaw vs. Keuchel, Part II—instantly became mission critical. Drop it, and the Astros would have to survive in Los Angeles for two elimination games against a 104-win team. But win Game 5—anyway, anyhow—and a long-elusive World Series trophy would clearly be within the Astros' grasp.

"If you had told me in spring training it would be a best-of-three to win the World Series, I would have said, 'I'm in,'" Springer said. "This is what you play for. Obviously, we didn't get the result here. But this is awesome. I'm so happy to be here. But the job isn't done, and I understand that."

The Astros' first spring training game had been played on February 25. Their regular season started April 3. They had been the best team in baseball, slumped through August, then been revived by Verlander's addition and inspired by Houston's resilience after Hurricane Harvey. Game 1 of the World Series had been rough. Game 4 was tougher. But even with a fractured bullpen, the Astros were still promised one more game at home and had already proven they were just as good as the Dodgers on the sport's biggest stage. There was no time to look back and reflect. Hinch's Astros could only push ahead.

"I don't have a lot of time to worry about burnout. We've got three games to win two, to try to win the World Series," Hinch said. "So I think encouragement goes a long way. You've got to stick to guys. We've got to get 27 outs, one way or another. I don't care who gets them. Our guys don't care who gets them. I think the comfortable roles and knowing who you're going to face and what the game situation is going to be in, it's just so unpredictable in this sport, especially at this stage of the year. So our guys are mentally tough enough to do it. Again, we come in and get big outs...and we get a 3–2 lead, our guys will be on cloud nine on the flight going to L.A., trying to win the World Series."

Game 5 was waiting. The best game in Astros history was about to be played.

16

IT'S YOUR TIME

[Playing for Houston] definitely has driven us. I think when it was all going on and we were on the road, and people's families were back here and you saw the stories, people lost everything during that thing. And when we got back home, a lot of us donated our time and got to meet and shake some hands. You see people who lost a lot. So this has been just historic that we can come back to the city and shine a positive light, as far as playing for them.

—Astros catcher Brian McCann

IT WAS NEVER over, until it was finally finished. And for as perfect as it all ended up—beautiful, majestic, indescribable—it began as a total mess.

Game 2 would have been enough. One heck of a World Series. The eventual winner (and loser) of the 2017 Fall Classic always possessing an unbelievable contest they could fall back on, telling future generations and baseball believers about the game you just could not believe unless you were fortunate enough to have played in it or watched with your own eyes.

Then Game 5 happened. It lasted an inning less than the 7–6 Astros win in 11 innings at Dodger Stadium in Game 2; Dallas Keuchel and Clayton Kershaw were both knocked out early. But the Houston Astros and Los Angeles Dodgers needed 14 combined pitchers just to reach 10 frames, and there were 25 runs, 28 hits, 11 walks, seven home runs, two errors, and 417 pitches in a single game on October 29. By the time that Derek Fisher—rookie, backup outfielder, pinch runner—slid across home plate, clapped his hands together, and shouted toward the screaming stands, five hours and 17 minutes had passed at Minute Maid Park, and the Astros were just one win away from winning the World Series.

"Just when I thought I could describe Game 2 as my favorite game of all time, I think Game 5 exceeded that and more," Astros manager A.J. Hinch said. "It's hard to put into words all the twists and turns in that game. The emotion; doing it at home in front of our home crowd. Just exactly what you expect to come to the park with Keuchel and Kershaw pitching—just a perfect setup game for a bunch of runs."

They tried to describe it. But they knew as soon as the fever dream was over that they'd spend the entire off-season trying to process it—and Game 6 was still to come.

Alex Bregman, Astros third baseman and author of Game 5's game-winning hit in the bottom of the 10th: "Before the game, I know that everybody knew that this was our last home game of the year. And that the people of Houston have been here with us the entire season, and they've stood strong through some tough times. And we were going to figure out a way to win this game for them."

Astros shortstop Carlos Correa: "It's crazy, man. To just be part of it is such a blessing. These games are hard on me. I feel like I'm going to have a heart attack out there every single time. It's high pressure out there. The game is going back and forth. Both teams are great, scoring runs, and putting up at-bats together. And there's a lot of pressure on you when you're out there and you want to win a game and you want to win the World Series."

Astros second baseman José Altuve: "The thing is, we never give up. It doesn't matter if we start the game [down] 4–0, but we keep playing, we keep putting some really good at-bats together. We came back twice, we took the lead, they tied the game, and we did it again. This is the team we are. This is the team we've been all season long. And I'm really proud of every single guy in that clubhouse, because tonight everybody did something to help us win the game."

Dodgers manager Dave Roberts: "This whole series has been an emotional roller-coaster. It's the two best teams playing for a championship. And these are two teams that play 27 outs....So you're not going to expect those guys to lay down. And obviously, you saw what our guys did tonight, and competed until the last out."

George Springer, hoarse and covered in sweat and dirt at 1:17 AM Houston time, tried to explain everything his Astros were feeling. His body was pulsing adrenaline, and he knew it was impossible to truly capture and define everything that had just happened. Heck, did it really happen? "This has been the best time of my baseball life," said Springer, who went 2-for-3 with a solo home run, three runs, three walks, and an RBI.

As the buzzing but exhausted Astros headed toward their clubhouse for the last time in 2017, departing fans wooed and screamed in a nearby hallway. The second-longest game in World Series history had also been one of the best since the Fall Classic began more than a century ago.

"That just happened! That just happened!" yelled an Astros fan, still accepting the terms of a new reality.

The Astros' final game at Minute Maid Park in 2017 became the peak point in 56 years of franchise history. Two World Series wins at the last moment in a five-day, cross-country span—after going 55 years without a single victory—left even the primary participants drained. The human heart and brain can only take so much.

"I'm ready to go home and sit on the couch and eat some food and just attempt to slow my brain down and just hang out," said Springer, who joked he would watch a show called "The Inside of My Eyelids."

Cy Young Award winners Keuchel and Kershaw could not last in Game 5. The latter gave up six runs in just $4\frac{2}{3}$ innings as his

October blues returned. But even though they knocked out Kershaw, the Astros were down 3–0 in the first, 4–0 in the fourth, 7–4 in the fifth, and 8–7 in the seventh. Then they watched a 12–9 lead in the ninth somehow disappear. Each time, someone in orange and blue came through. Yuli Gurriel, Altuve, Springer—after allowing a ball to roll all the way to the center-field wall, erasing a 7–7 tie—and Correa all lifted up the Astros during a win that defined their season.

"Yeah, five-hour game, but it doesn't matter. I can play a 10-hour game if we are going to win. That's the most important thing, to win the game," Altuve said. "We have one more victory. But we're still very humble about that. We also know who we're playing. You have to play for every single inning to beat the Dodgers. We've beat them in L.A. We've got to do it again."

The 23-year-old Bregman, who went over the Green Monster to set up the ALDS clincher against Boston at Fenway Park, stepped up to the plate in the 10th inning of Game 5. Once-feared Dodgers closer Kenley Jansen offered a first-pitch, two-out cutter at 92 mph. Bregman smoothly lined the ball to left-center field, pushing Fisher—from second base, pinch running for Brian McCann—across home. After all the homers, comebacks, blown leads, and last-breath rallies, Bregman simply ended it, thus starting the post-midnight dance party in downtown Houston.

"Springer had a huge at-bat and walked right before me. And I took one more swing on the on-deck circle, and I looked to Correa. Correa said, 'It's your time,'" said Bregman, who was screaming and pointing at everyone still on the field and in the stands as it approached 1:00 AM at Minute Maid Park.

During 21 combined tense-and-tight innings in Games 2 and 5, the Astros had perfected what they first started creating with all their walkoffs in 2015. The game was never over until it was finished. They always kept fighting, just because fighting back is always fun.

"Just pure joy," Bregman said. "Because when you look around you and you see the smiles on your teammates' face, it makes everything worth it. It makes every weight that you lifted in the off-season, every swing that you took in the cage [worth it]. When you feel like you came through for your team and you see the joy on their faces, there's nothing like it. It's such a special feeling that I'm so fortunate and blessed to feel today. It's an unbelievable moment.... You dream about it as a little kid. To be living a dream, one win away from the World Series, is really special."

After Game 5, the Astros and Dodgers had already set a World Series record for combined home runs (22). During the constantly back-and-forth thriller, every straightforward storyline was torched. And by the fifth inning—Altuve blasting a two-out, three-run homer 415 feet to center field to tie the game at 7–7; Minute Maid Park cranked to its loudest volume of the year—it was clear that the winner of Game 5 was going to be the team that could survive the longest, then finally end a battle that would not stop.

"I'd say everybody is pretty tired now, but we won't be that tired when we show up in L.A.," Bregman said. "I'll say this: I thought Game 2 was probably the best baseball game I ever played in. It was unbelievable, the huge homer and all the home runs that were hit. I didn't think that would ever be topped—I thought that would be the best game I ever played in my career. Who knows where this one ranks? Right up there with that game. Back and forth, the two best teams in baseball fighting to the very end and going toe to toe with each other. Everybody was used on both teams, pretty much, every single player. It was special for us to come out on top."

With 11th- and 10th-inning, come-from-behind wins in the book, the team that had never won a World Series game before 2017 was just one more win away from the trophy, thanks to the craziness—good, contagious, redeeming craziness—that was Game 5.

"The first thing we're going to do is get some sleep," Hinch said. "Have a quick turnaround and get on the plane to L.A. We've got a long travel day tomorrow. It's still a one-game season. We're going to walk in and try to win the game in Game 6. We've got [Justin] Verlander going, coming off this big win. Our team is pretty good at building off this type of momentum. It's a singular focus on trying to win the next game. For our guys, we know what's at stake—they know what's at stake. This is Game 6 of the World Series coming up. How much prep work do you really need to get yourself ready to play?"

Some would barely be called upon in the season's final month. Others no longer made the cut, despite helping the best team in the American League reach baseball's final stage. Mike Fiers started 28 games, won eight, and threw 153$\frac{1}{3}$ innings for the 2017 Astros. Jake Marisnick had 230 at-bats. Cameron Maybin was actually hotter than Justin Verlander for a few days. Tony Sipp pitched in 46 games. But only Maybin took the field for the Astros during the playoffs, and that was just for five at-bats before Game 6 back in Los Angeles. With only 25 spots allowed on the postseason roster for each round, some Astros who helped carry the club during the early months of the 2017 season were now forced to watch as an instantly memorable World Series became more dramatic with each passing game.

"We want guys who have been on this team for a long period of time to be with us all, to be a part of this. But there's only 25 spots," Hinch said. "It is hard. I'm sure it's hard for them, to want to be a part of this on the active side. But they deserve every opportunity to soak this up and be a part of it, because everybody's contribution counts at a lot of different levels."

Fisher had been called upon at the perfect time. The rookie outfielder made his major league debut on June 14, when the Astros were first being hit by critical injuries. By the end of the regular season, the 2014 first-round pick had hit five home runs and knocked in 17 runs while scoring 21 in 53 games. But in the playoffs, Fisher only appeared in five games and never recorded an at-bat. His lone scored run changed the World Series, though. When Bregman lined a single to left field at the end of Game 5, a rookie little seen in the playoffs gave the Astros a 3–2 series lead.

"It just shows what it takes for a team to get this far," Fisher said. "Obviously, our core lineup is as good as it gets. But when you look at the great teams, there's guys that are able to help whenever they can."

The Astros' increased depth, in the lineup and on the mound, became a tipping point in 2017. Opposing arms could no longer wait until the bottom of the order to slice through free-swinging, strikeout-prone bats and soak up easy outs. No one felt the dividing line between the regular season and playoffs more than Marisnick. After hitting .243 with 16 home runs and an .815 OPS during 106 games from April 3 through September 13, Marisnick fractured his thumb. His legs were ready for the World Series, but Marisnick's inability to swing a bat left a key regular-season Astro on the outside looking in during the Fall Classic. Marisnick remained close to his team regularly throughout the playoffs, though. And as Game 5 proved with Fisher's final run, every name—big and small—mattered for the Astros in 2017.

"At some point, it's going to take all 40 guys on a 40-man roster to win a championship," Maybin said. "That doesn't mean everybody is going to be there at the end. It doesn't mean everybody was there at the beginning. But it takes a roll, it takes a collective group not only getting to the playoffs, but making it here and having a chance to accomplish a wonderful feat."

Game 6 belonged to the Astros' ace for five innings. Verlander was erasing the Dodgers. Springer followed up his team's Game 5 home-run heroics with a solo shot early in Game 6. Houston's baseball team was just 12 outs away from winning the World Series, back at ear-pounding Dodger Stadium on October 31.

It ended up as 3–1 Los Angeles on the next-to-last night of baseball in 2017. The Astros and Dodgers were left staring at a final, season-defining Game 7. How the Astros reacted to the deflating loss said everything about what they would eventually pull off. They were disappointed, knowing they had let a major opportunity slip away. Verlander on the mound in a title clincher? Finish the Dodgers off. But Hinch's team also sounded as confident and driven as ever inside a cramped visitor's clubhouse. Play from February through October, and it all comes down to one final game? Who would not take that? It would be the Astros' second Game 7 in 11 days. They had won the first one and were already mentally preparing for the next.

"If you carry any baggage into Game 7 of the World Series, then you're certainly misguided with your attention," Hinch said. "We will come as positive as ever, ready to play. It is what looks to be one of the most exhilarating games that we're ever going to be a part of. Who can guarantee that you're going to be in Game 7 ever again? Come ready to play. Have your best attitude, have your best opportunity."

Correa returned to the backyard imagination of a child. Dreaming big and picturing everything being on the line. One game—and maybe one player—deciding a season and history for two 100-plus win teams.

"It's the last game of the season, for sure," Correa said. "We want it to be the best."

Through six games, the Astros and Dodgers had battered each other in instant classics and fought through tight, tense contests that drained fans' hearts. For the third time in four years, MLB would need the full seven to crown a champion.

"I've been part of two of the best games that I've ever played in, and they've both been in [this] World Series. That's pretty special," said Verlander, who allowed two runs and three hits while striking out nine in his first loss as an Astro. "No matter what, this series is going down in the history books as one of the best series of all-time. I think [Wednesday] is going to be nothing short of spectacular."

McCullers acknowledged the series was heading toward Game 7 ever since Game 1. A fiery 24-year-old born for big moments was about to take the mound with a world championship on the line.

"The guys know in the clubhouse that I go out there and I'm not going to hold anything back. I think they understand that I'm willing to give everything I have for the guys behind me and the guys in the dugout," McCullers said. "That's something that I've always tried to pride myself on, regardless of how I'm pitching or how I'm feeling....Always having those guys know that I'm going to go out there and give them everything I have. So I think that's where their confidence in me, just going out there and being able to compete, comes from."

Hinch always kept his Astros cool. Fiery, passionate, and highly competitive. But cool. He was supposed to be a numbers guy—and he was. But when Hinch stuck with Brad Peacock through almost four innings of scoreless extended relief in Game 3 of the World Series, the Astros manager went off personal feel as much as he did pregame charts and advanced statistics.

Since 2015 Hinch had been the perfect manager for the rebuilt Astros. During the 2017 playoffs, he'd been under the microscope for almost a month. He was human, so there had been public missteps. He had also managed his team as well as humanly possible and perfectly set the tone—backing Springer, standing behind Charlie Morton and McCullers, gradually piecing together his cracked bullpen—from Game 1 of the ALDS. Hinch used a variety of modern and old-school techniques, all while standing up for his own beliefs. And at the heart of the 2017 Astros' thrilling on-field style and addicting personality was Hinch's ever-growing relationship with his team, which had only strengthened since 2015.

"He lets us play, he lets us have fun, he lets us do our thing and play the way that we're used to," Marwin González said. "But whenever we do something bad or something that he doesn't like, he will wait after the game and call us up in private and then try to talk about it. He's really good about that."

Hinch had spent three long baseball years building and maintaining all his different relationships within the Astros. As the final game of the World Series waited, the bonds he had created and belief he had placed in his players would be tested one more time in 2017.

"You have to be honest with your players and you can support them in different ways," Hinch said. "One of them is by continuing to provide opportunity, and one of them is to encourage. Sometimes it's to have private, tough conversations with them. But this game's about players, and you can't blindly support—there has to be some content behind it. When you communicate and develop a trusting bond, then you can have both good and bad conversations."

In the hours before Game 7, Hinch's team was already saying all the right things about winning the World Series in Los Angeles.

17

FOREVER SPECIAL

It's unbelievable. It's indescribable. When you get to spring, you know who you have, you see what you have, and there's always that thought of "We could do it," but the 162-plus games is a lot of games. And a lot of things have to go right in order to get here. And our team believed in each other all year...through the good times and the bad times, through a rough stretch in August to getting down 3–2 against a very good New York team. There's a lot of things that happened. And this is—I'm so happy to be a part of it, to bring a championship back to a city that desperately needed one—is a surreal feeling.

—Astros outfielder George Springer

THE SKY WAS bright blue. Big white clouds stretched above palm trees and hills. U2's "One" blended into the Eagles' "Hotel California," then became the Beatles' "Here Comes the Sun" on Dodger Stadium's blaring speakers.

Houston was in Game 7 of the World Series. And it was not just a misplaced pregame feeling, caught up in the buzz of Los Angeles. The calm, cool Astros insisted they were ready—Game 6 was over; one final winnable game remained—and then showed it the moment that the pageantry of the 2017 Fall Classic disappeared.

"Our team is as balanced and aware as any team I've ever been around. When the last out was recorded last night, our players in the dugout had a tremendous vibe about them. They've moved onto Game 7 already," said manager A.J. Hinch, before Lance

McCullers Jr. faced Yu Darvish in the final game of 2017. "We know what's at stake. We know the importance. Nobody hung their head. We're playing in one of the most epic World Series in history. And I think our players have appreciation for that. We want to win. We're going to do everything we can today to win. But we're not letting the emotional angst get the best of us, from Game 1 all the way through Game 7. So I didn't need to say anything to them other than encourage them, keep the mood upbeat. The players were already doing that from the last out last night."

A victory would give the Astros a true dream season—"storybook," as Hinch called it. A defeat would still set up Hinch's club as early World Series favorites in 2018. But for the third-year manager, thinking past November 1 was impossible as the hours before Game 7 narrowed down. The Astros were playing their 213th game of the year, counting spring training, regular season, and postseason. Just one more win would represent total validation of the master plan that general manager Jeff Luhnow had begun laying out almost six years ago.

"I can appreciate [the World Series] more if we win. I'll appreciate the heck out of it," Hinch said. "But I think as time will go by and we'll watch the DVDs that are made of this series and the memories that are built from this series, there will be a great appreciation of where it fits in the context of history of baseball. But right now in the middle of it, we just want to win. There are moments when you can take a step back and smile and see what you're a part of. But for the most part, it's focused on what we're doing now."

The "now" started before there was a single out. George Springer doubled down the left-field line, locking onto an 84-mph Darvish slider. Alex Bregman reached on a throwing error, which pushed Springer across the plate for the night's first run. When the first frame was over, it was 2–0 Astros. By the end of the second, it was 5–0 road team, with Darvish's evening over ($1\frac{2}{3}$ innings, three hits, four earned runs) and the American League's best team playing like a world champion from the start.

"You have to pick a pitch. You have to find an area of the zone that you feel comfortable with and stay in the strike zone the most you can. If he gets you to chase, it's advantage Darvish. If he gets you to hit his off-speed pitches, it's advantage Darvish," Hinch said. "So you have to be very disciplined. And we did that two games in a row, where we got hittable pitches and did damage. In the first game there was a lot of extra-base hits, and we drove in some runs. Today, George delivered the big blow at the end. But how we scored our first couple of runs of just manufacturing runs against a top-end pitcher like that, our plan was to make it tough on him and give good, tough at-bats, because we didn't know how long he was going to be in....Before the game, we stood behind second base and said, 'You might only get one at-bat against Darvish.' Now, I didn't know that was going to be because we scored a lot of runs. I thought it was going to be just how creative they were going to get."

Dodgers manager Dave Roberts struggled to explain Darvish's sudden fall. A dangerous, multi-pitch right-hander—who used to own the Astros when he was a Ranger—ended up 0–2 in the World Series with an abysmal 21.60 ERA, allowing nine hits and nine runs (eight earned) in just 3⅓ innings, while giving up two home runs and two walks and striking out none.

"Just unexpected, even today, the velocity," Roberts said. "I thought he was right there. I thought he was going to really throw the baseball well. And I think it was three-and-a-third, maybe, in this series and just very unfortunate. I know he wanted the baseball. I know he was prepared. I just can't explain the results. I really can't."

The Astros did not score again in Game 7. They also did not have to. Brad Peacock, Francisco Liriano, Chris Devenski, and Charlie Morton backed McCullers for a combined six-hit, one-run evening. Springer homered for the fifth time in the series, capturing the Fall Classic MVP. Then orange rushed the field in a stadium of silenced blue. It was 5–1 Astros in Game 7 of the World Series in the electric L.A. night. Down went the Dodgers. Long live a baseball team that captured Houston's heart and inspired a city that was still recovering from the destruction of Hurricane Harvey.

"The wildness of this series, the wackiness of this series, the emotional ups and downs," Springer said. "Being able to play in this is something that I will never, ever forget, even if this is the only time I will ever get here."

Just two months after the greatest natural disaster in the city's history had flooded right field at Minute Maid Park, the 2017 Astros—Altuve, Correa, Springer, Bregman, Verlander, Keuchel, McCullers, Morton, Giles, and the rest—had captured the first World Series title in franchise history. Six years after losing 106 games—then 107, then 111—the rebuilt Astros were world champions, ahead of schedule and with their supremely talented young core just beginning to reach the first stage of its potential.

Altuve had lived and played through it all. Now the best hitter in baseball was on the best team in the sport. "We got to the playoffs in 2015," Altuve said. "Very young team, we didn't have that much experience. We couldn't go further. But last year we had another great year. I think it was a good year—we didn't clinch, but it was another good year. And then this year in spring training I realized, like, this is the team. It's something in our clubhouse....A lot of chemistry, good relationships between players, coaches....I kind of believed it was the year. Everybody did it, and now we're here."

As the trophy with all the flags was raised toward a stadium-lights-lit sky, Evan Gattis started crying. Jeff Bagwell (Hall of Famer) and Correa (the future) proudly hugged each other. It was over and finally done. After 55 seasons of always falling short, the Astros had won it all.

"To get our first world championship with this group of guys, it's just a tremendous group of kids," said Bagwell, who entered the Hall of Fame in the same year the Astros won the World Series. "They loved each other. Even when things went bad, they still found a way to come back. I'm very, very proud of them, proud of the city and certainly very proud of this organization."

Astros president Reid Ryan, Nolan's son, just let the tears flow. Houston—world champs. "This is for everybody who's ever worn this uniform," said Ryan, as his eyes kept filling with joy. "I was born here. I watched my dad play here. I watched all those games. The Astros' DNA is in me. And seeing these guys accomplish something that no one's ever been able to accomplish…I'm just so happy for them."

Hinch's Astros became the first team to ever beat the storied Boston Red Sox and legendary New York Yankees in the same playoffs. Then there was the Hollywood magic of Game 2 of the World Series and the insanity that was five hours and 17 minutes during Game 5 at Minute Maid Park. Finally, taking the first-ever World Series Game 7 at Dodger Stadium by overcoming mighty Los Angeles, which featured the highest price tag in baseball and entered the postseason as the best team in the game.

"Going through Boston, going through New York, coming through Los Angeles, and winning the World Series, it's pretty unbelievable," Hinch said.

Astros fans, waiting on a championship since 1962, started counting outs as soon as it was 5–0 road team in the second inning. The final out—Corey Seager bouncing a 96-mph sinker to Altuve, who threw to a joyous Yuli Gurriel—became an instant celebration. After Houston's baseball team won the 2017 world title, Correa proposed to his girlfriend and was engaged on the Dodger Stadium field.

It was not the Chicago Cubs and a drought that lasted 108 years. But it was the Astros, and Houston's championship was a long time coming. For a city that had struggled so many times to win the real thing—late, crushing heartbreaks and unbelievable letdowns—taking the world title in the year of Harvey only made the dream that more real.

"It was an emotional journey just getting here," Gattis said. "I'm just talking about this postseason. I'm not talking about my life. I'm just talking about the last month. It just feels like completion, man."

Springer, who struggled to even put together a good swing in Game 1, was named the World Series MVP. He hit .379 with five home runs, seven RBIs, eight runs, five walks, and a 1.471 OPS. The leadoff hitter whom Hinch had backed had capped the Astros' Game 2 turnaround, then ignited Game 7 before finishing 2-for-5 with a double, home run, and two RBIs in the final contest of 2017.

"He does a great job in figuring out his players, figuring out what makes them work individually," Springer said. "And A.J., to his credit, with me kind of all year, just told me to go play. Don't try to do too much. Don't get ahead of yourself. Go out and kind of enjoy the game. And after Game 1 he sent me a text and just said to kind of enjoy this, because this is the best time of our baseball life. And he stuck with me. He stuck by me. And I will run through a wall for that guy any day."

The names, numbers, and moments would always be remembered: Verlander, Altuve, Springer, Correa, and Bregman in 2017. The season-altering dates: August 31, when Verlander became an Astro at the last minute; September 2, when baseball returned to Houston after Harvey; November 1, when the Astros claimed the world championship in Game 7 in the L.A. night. Hinch had guided it all. Jim Crane and Luhnow had built it, constructing the best team in baseball from the remnants of a fallen franchise that was intentionally torn apart in 2011. All were forever linked with the best team in Astros history—the first to win it all.

"There are so many people who have built this team," Hinch said. "And, obviously, Jeff and his staff have done a tremendous job."

The owner and GM of the rebuild had accomplished what they first set out to do at the end of 2011. Six years after a massive rebuild began, the Astros were world champions. They were also set up to be annual contenders for years. "We took a lot of heat early, but we were ready for that," Crane said. "It's magical it all came together. It happened in a short five or six years. But it seems like 100 every day when you're getting your butt kicked at 100 [losses]. But now we flipped that around, and I'm just so happy for the guys."

National TV interviews, *Saturday Night Live*, and a constant stream of media appearances followed. The fun, thrilling, easily likable Astros were a perfect advertisement for baseball's much-changed modern world. But the real celebration took place in the city the Astros called home.

In 2015 fans were gradually convinced to return to the ball-park and give their hearts to their local team. In 2017 Houston could not get enough of the Astros, and the city spent October and November drenched in orange and blue.

"This team will always be remembered as the 2017 World Series champions. They can't take that away from any of us," Springer said.

Hinch initially took the trophy home and slept next to it, then brought it to breakfast as he joined former Astros manager Phil Garner. McCullers returned home from Los Angeles to find his street decorated with balloons, orange-and-blue streamers, and No. 43 pumpkins. "It means a lot to us as players," he said. "But the city has waited so long and it had to endure so much heart-break along the way....To be able to bring the first championship to Houston is going to be forever special."

Luhnow reflected on a lasting image captured by the *Houston Chronicle*: Astros fans watching the World Series inside a bare, gutted room after Hurricane Harvey. "Every year we ask the city and the fan base to rally around the team," Hinch said. "And it's okay for a fan base to ask a team to rally around them. And I think I saw our players step up...and obviously gather some sort of energy, some extra motivation. We wore a patch—nothing better than Springer patting his chest when he hit the home run, after we'd come back from the hurricane. Somehow, some way that connects communities."

The community united one more time for an overwhelming parade that would not be forgotten. Houston mayor Sylvester Turner, Keuchel, Correa, and Crane stood together in a confetti-covered fire truck. Craig Biggio and Bagwell proudly sat together like kids, then Biggio stood tall in downtown Houston with his arms raised to the sky. There were endless photos, constant screams and cheers, and so many people that some stood in trees while others filled parking garages, just for a glimpse of their world champion Astros.

For two key lesser names, the final crowning in Houston held a strong personal touch. Two days after Game 7 in Los Angeles, Chris Devenski had reached a stage that once seemed unobtainable. "It's tough to believe," the reliever said. "I always imagined something like this happening. But sometimes I felt like imagination can only take you so far....For it to really happen is unbelievable."

Then there was Charlie Morton, opening up before the city opened up its streets and arms to the Astros. "It still hasn't sunk in yet that we won the whole thing," the Game 7 winner said. "Obviously, I know we did. But the ramifications and that reality hasn't really set in yet." Houston's baseball team would not have made it to the World Series without August 31 and Verlander. But once the Astros arrived on baseball's grandest stage, it took a final push from a 33-year-old right-hander to finally put the club over the top. "This guy's the biggest steal of the [last] off-season," Bregman said.

That was how the rebuilt Astros had done it. Their way. Defying convention, enduring criticism, and then proving just how right they were. A playoff ace acquired just in time for an unbelievable postseason. Stars internally developed, improving year after year. Critical arms and bats that baseball's other teams passed on.

Altuve, Springer, and Hinch lifted up a trophy for everyone to see. The people filled up their city, longing to see their world champions.

18

ANYTHING IS POSSIBLE

There were so many parts of that season, it's hard to say that all parts were the best. As much as I look back at the impact, I don't want to call the hurricane the best year of my life. It's a story for us, but it's a reality for so many people in the city.... But it's the most proud I've ever been in baseball.

—A.J. Hinch

JOSÉ ALTUVE WON the American League MVP in the year that the Houston Astros won the World Series. That tells you anything and everything was possible for A.J. Hinch's baseball team in 2017.

Altuve was a 5'6" second baseman from Venezuela who had initially been ignored, then fought through three consecutive 100-plus-loss seasons to become the best overall hitter in major league baseball. A vote that was supposed to be close ultimately was not: Altuve received 405 points and 27 of 30 first-place MVP votes, while New York Yankees rookie slugger Aaron Judge finished second with 279 points and only two first-place votes. Altuve was no longer underrated. The heart and soul of the Astros was now recognized as one of the most talented players in the entire sport.

Old-school athleticism, tradition, and common sense had dominated modern power and hype. Batting average mattered, as did the throwback value of playing hard every single day.

The AL MVP award—just the second MVP honor in franchise history—was the final peak for the greatest Astros season in team history. Not bad for a 16-year-old who was told he should leave when he first attended an international tryout with the Astros. "It's hard to believe....They told me not to come back," Altuve said. "But there was something in me and my dad. He went with me that day, and we were like, 'Okay, we have to go again. We've got to try again.' Normally, when they tell you not to go, you stop—you stop trying. And maybe I should try another team. But I was like, 'No, I want to go again. I want to go to this tryout again because I feel like I can make something happen.' And now 10 years later, I'm a World Series champion....And now three weeks after that, I'm an American League MVP."

He was also on an early Hall of Fame pace. After 982 regular-season games, Altuve had more hits (1,250), home runs (84), RBIs (403), and stolen bases (231), and a higher batting average (.316) and OPS (.816) than MLB hit-king Pete Rose did at the same time in his career. "I think I'm the smallest player in the big leagues, and I'm like 160 pounds, so I'm not too strong," Altuve said. "That's what I love about baseball. They give the opportunity to every single guy to develop and play the game. There's not a rule that you have to be six-foot or you have to be real strong to play baseball and to become a good player."

The Astros had finally been a great team in 2017. Before a new year arrived and World Series memories turned into spring training plans, Hinch set out to again thank the young men who had played so hard and accomplished so much for him. With a world title forever in the Astros' possession, Hinch made one more connection with his championship team. The manager played Santa Claus during the holiday season, hand-delivering personalized bottles of championship-branded wine to the players who delivered from early February in West Palm Beach, Florida, to November 1 during that unforgettable night at Dodger Stadium.

"I really just wanted to say thanks to all of them for what they did to contribute," said Hinch, who kept game balls and lineup cards from the Astros' four World Series wins as personal keep-sakes. "Obviously, the rings are going to be the biggest prize; the memories will never go away—all the different things that are going on with our team. But, for me, I tried to think of something to do to give them a small little memory and just a little thank you."

As for his personal souvenirs?

"There's probably a lot of stories on that game card that only I know," Hinch said. "Those cards I'll keep forever, alongside those simple game balls."

The World Series–winning manager—Hinch held a 271–215 regular-season record and .558 winning percentage after three seasons in Houston—also kept his family close with him throughout the playoffs. And as the Astros celebrated their first title in the Los Angeles night, Hinch paused everything to connect with his father, who had taught him the game and first ignited his love of the sport.

"One of my best memories from the World Series is, I'm on the stage and I have the trophy and I'm surrounded by our team," Hinch said. "Jeff [Luhnow] is there, Jim [Crane] is there, Reid Ryan is there....And I took a moment and just looked up at the sky. And somebody got a picture of it and sent it to me on my phone. And, again, one of those things that only I know was going on at that moment. I'll cherish that picture forever."

The manager of the 2017 Astros knew how powerful and life-changing it all was. He had stood on the stage in the perfect, glowing L.A. night and felt all the joy. But it was not until Hinch settled back in Houston that the full realization sank in.

"Post–World Series, whether it's recognition or appreciation or just interaction with our fans, I've realized kind of the magnitude of what we did within the city, within the fan base," Hinch said. "The championship resonates with so many Houstonians, young and old. And being the first Astros championship even multiplies that. So I've felt the love and support from virtually everybody I've run into."

Three months later, the Astros were back at it. Carlos Correa, George Springer, Alex Bregman, and Altuve returned to West Palm Beach, Florida, for another spring training. Justin Verlander was a full-season Astro for the first time. Hinch had to figure out how much freedom he could still give his world champions in February, and how much he had to push a team that had gone so far not that long ago.

Altuve was a season away from being in the final year of his team-friendly contract. But, of course, there would be no settling for the 2017 American League MVP as a new season approached. At 8:15 AM daily, Altuve and Correa put in extra work on a turf field as the morning sun rose, working on positioning, throwing, and double-play drills that the duo hoped would create outs and change the outcomes of games in 2018. Two of the Astros' brightest stars were united in trying to discover an extra half-second of athleticism that would become an advantage.

As Dallas Keuchel entered his final year before free agency and Lance McCullers Jr. set a goal of making every scheduled start during his fourth MLB season, prospects tried to crack one of the deepest rosters in the sport. And even when Yuli Gurriel was lost to hand surgery in late February, the Astros had enough extra pieces to initially overcome the loss of a sweet-hitting first baseman who gloved the final out of the 2017 World Series.

The world champions also had a new weapon. After going through years where they constantly dealt away major league names to stockpile prospects, the Astros had entered a new era. Verlander moved his baseball life to Houston when the Astros dealt away three minor leaguers. Four months later, a rebuilding Pittsburgh team shipped right-hander Gerrit Cole to the Astros in exchange for three role players and a minor leaguer.

Cole had been the No. 1 overall pick of the 2011 draft, during a year when the plummeting Astros went through their first of three 100-loss seasons and a franchise that would soon be rebuilt took Springer at No. 11. Almost seven years later, the Pirates were tearing it down and turning Cole—the ace of a 98-win Pittsburgh club in 2015, who went 19–8 with a 2.60 ERA, 1.09 WHIP, and 202 strikeouts in 208 innings that year—into the Astros' No. 4 spring starter, behind Verlander, Keuchel, and McCullers in the rotation.

Tanking was also the cool, new thing in baseball. A sport that was often slow to change played follow-the-leader after the reconstructed Chicago Cubs and Astros won it all. As spring training played out and Game 1 of the 2018 season approached, Major League Baseball and the MLB Players Association engaged in a public battle that echoed the stances of franchises during previous rebuilding periods. Too many teams were following the mindsets of the 111-loss Astros from 2013 and the 101-loss Cubs from 2012, and big-name players were still out of work.

"A record number of talented free agents remain unemployed in an industry where revenues and franchise values are at record highs," MLBPA executive director Tony Clark said in a statement. "Spring training has always been associated with hope for a new season. This year, a significant number of teams are engaged in a race to the bottom. This conduct is a fundamental breach of the trust between a team and its fans, and threatens the very integrity of our game."

The rise of sabermetrics and modern player evaluation had changed the game. Why give Free Agent A $80 million for five years when you could pay the league minimum for comparable production from Players B, C, and D and have them under team control for years? The Astros accepted that outlook in 2012 and 2013 as their rebuild bottomed out.

MLB backed the Astros then and stood its ground the year after Houston won the world title. "Owners own teams for one reason: they want to win. In baseball, it has always been true that clubs go through cyclical, multiyear strategies directed at winning," MLB said in a statement. "It is common at this point in the calendar to have large numbers of free agents unsigned. What is uncommon is to have some of the best free agents sitting unsigned, even though they have substantial offers, some in nine figures....To lay responsibility on the clubs for the failure of some agents to accurately assess the market is unfair, unwarranted, and inflammatory."

As March drew near, the MLBPA filed a grievance against the Oakland Athletics, Miami Marlins, Tampa Bay Rays, and Pirates, accusing the organizations of failing to appropriately spend revenue-sharing money. Tampa Bay had traded Evan Longoria, Jake Odorizzi, Corey Dickerson, and Steven Souza Jr. Miami had slashed payroll and was rebuilding yet again—this time with Derek Jeter calling the shots—sending away Giancarlo Stanton, Dee Gordon, Christian Yelich, and Marcell Ozuna. Pittsburgh had shipped out 2013 MVP Andrew McCutchen days after sending Cole to Houston.

With the Astros' core, chemistry, and culture intact—a retired Carlos Beltran highlighted the few off-season depletions—prospects now struggled to find an open space on the team's loaded roster. The flickering hope that used to carry fans through the dark years of the rebuild had now been replaced by a major league reality. Nearly five years after Springer first teased his MLB power with two long home-run blasts in a spring-training blowout, the defending World Series champions were deeper than ever as they began their 2018 exhibition campaign. The lineup was stacked, the rotation was overflowing, an improved bullpen had multiple options, and the bench barely had room.

MVP, Cy Young Award, Silver Slugger, and Gold Glove winners walked into the clubhouse daily, striding through a hallway that displayed oversized framed photos of franchise-defining championship moments. A driven team that embraced the potential for a World Series repeat went to work daily at the newly named FITTEAM Ballpark of the Palm Beaches, which now featured an oversized "2017 World Champions" logo above the left-field wall and a smaller version of the symbol near the entryway to the Astros' clubhouse.

Smiling fans posed for family photos in front of the huge white H and orange star. Teenagers took selfies and held up the No. 1 sign, while autograph seekers waited for hours in the sun for a shot to have an item inked by one of the Astros' many stars. Inside a sparkling spring stadium, stacks of T-shirts, hats, and programs bore proof of the team's world title. And on the first official day of the gradual march toward Opening Day, a banner was dropped and fireworks went off as the Astros showed off their world championship logo.

On March 12, Hinch's club was honored at the White House. A week later, Altuve received a franchise-record $151 million contract extension that featured a no-trade clause, potentially keeping him in an Astros uniform through 2024.

After taking three of four games from the Rangers in Arlington to open their 2018 campaign as MLB's reigning world champions, the Astros celebrated the initial two days of their home-opening series by unveiling a golden 2017 championship banner above the left-field wall at Minute Maid Park, then presenting more than 1,300 shining rings to everyone from players and coaches to staff members and team employees.

"I'm extremely happy to be back in Houston and get to say hi to the boys," said Beltran, who rejoined his former teammates April 3 inside a roaring stadium. "Having an opportunity to be present at the ring ceremony is something that, as a ballplayer, I tried to chase that dream for a long time. And finally, thank God, that gave me the opportunity to receive it last year in my retirement year. So it's a very special day for me."

Hope, optimism, and annual renewal were clichés the Astros no longer relied upon. They did not have to fake it through the spring, then admit by May or June they knew they never had a chance.

It was Altuve, Correa, Springer, Bregman, Verlander, Keuchel, and many more in orange and blue. A team you dreamt of and planned for, just waiting for another chance to see the world champs up close again.

The rebuilt Astros had the makings of a real dynasty. After an unbelievable 2017 season, anything was possible for Houston's baseball team.

ACKNOWLEDGMENTS

THANKS to the Houston Chronicle, the newspaper's editors, and my colleagues.

ABOUT THE AUTHOR

BRIAN T. SMITH is a sports columnist for the *Houston Chronicle*. He has won multiple Associated Press Sports Editors awards and been honored by numerous journalism organizations. Smith previously covered the NFL, MLB, and NBA as a beat writer.